MW00388406

ANYONE
CAN SEE THE
LIGHT

ANYONE

CAN SEE THE

LIGHT

THE SEVEN KEYS TO A *GUIDED* OUT-OF-BODY EXPERIENCE

DIANNE MORRISSEY, PH.D.

✳ STILLPOINT PUBLISHING

✳ STILLPOINT PUBLISHING
Books to awaken the human spirit and build a society that
honors The Earth, Humanity, and The Sacred in All Life.

For a free catalog or ordering information, write
Stillpoint Publishing, Box 640, Walpole, NH 03608, USA
or call
1-800-847-4014 TOLL-FREE (Continental USA)
1-603-756-9281 (Foreign)

Text Copyright © 1996 by Dianne Morrissey, Ph.D.

This book is manufactured in the United States of America.

Cover design by Karen Savary
Text design by Heather Gendron

Published by Stillpoint Publishing, PO Box 640,
Meetinghouse Road, Walpole, NH 03608

ISBN: 1-883478-13-8

Library of Congress Catalog Card Number: #96-068200

1 3 5 7 9 8 6 4 2

**This book is printed on acid-free recycled paper
to save trees and help protect the Earth's ecology.**

To Dr. Thelma Moss
and Mr. John Hahn, for their
encouragement toward inner creativity

"One can't believe in impossible things."

"I daresay you haven't had much practice," said the Queen. "When I was your age, I always did it for half-an-hour a day. Why, sometimes I've believed as many as six impossible things before breakfast."

—Lewis Carroll, author of
Through the Looking Glass

Contents

Foreword

Are near-death experiences real? Dianne Morrissey, Ph.D., author of *Anyone Can See The Light*, does more than document their validity—she shows that we do not have to nearly die to have the equivalent of a near-death experience.

Recent research clearly documents that we will all have a spiritual vision at the point of death. This is no different than the type of vision which may occur in a variety of situations, from deep meditation and prayer to one with no trigger at all. One healthy young man I know had a "near-death" experience while in typing class!

Dr. Morrissey actually learned how to harness the power of the near-death vision. Her book takes the readers into exciting new territory by demonstrating how to have transformational out-of-body experiences just as powerful as those encountered when one is dying. These experiences will, however, occur while one is safely in the dream state.

No one is better qualified than Dr. Morrissey to present this breakthrough concept. She herself survived a powerful near-death experience: she was electrocuted and technically "dead" for twenty-five minutes. Dr. Morrissey has lectured to college and university audiences and continues to appear on the academic circuit. She is eagerly sought after by the media because she combines scholarly rigor with her own personal insights on near-death experiences.

It is an honor for me to introduce this book to the public. It represents a great advance in our understanding of near-death and out-of-body experiences. It is also a practical "how-to" manual that anyone can use successfully. I know, because after I read it, I tried her techniques—and they worked for me!

> — Dr. Melvin Morse, author of
> *Transformed by the Light* and
> *Closer to the Light*

Acknowledgments

ALL BOOKS ARE A COLLABORATIVE EFFORT, no matter who the author is, and my book is certainly no rare exception. It is here that I wish to applaud my contributors for their assistance.

First, I wish to express my heartfelt gratitude for those who shared their personal stories and their lives with me. I hope they will forgive my occasional condensation of their stories, which was sometimes necessary; these people provided the inner strength required for the completed work. They include Leah and her husband, Ellior, Elizabeth and her son, Doris, Helen, Bonnie, Charlotte, Cory, Johannah, Peter, Deborah, Enrique, Mathew, Travy, Johnny, Annabelle, Joseph, Tom and others.

I also owe a special thanks for the assistance of Linda and her daughter Tammi. My sincerest appreciation goes out to my friend, Rosanna for sharing her story and helping so many others.

I wish to thank Carmen, Paul, Mary Ann, Teri, Fiona, Charles, Beth, Cathe, Sally, Diana, Nicole, Jan, Don, Ofelia, Carol, Patti, Wendy, Laura, John, Linda, John, Deanne, Al, Maria, Ellen, John, Orea, Lynn and all the others who participated in sharing their experiences with me over the years. I have cited the occupations only of those who gave me permission to do so.

I also congratulate my husband for his patience in listening to me talk, sometimes endlessly, about dying. I wish to convey my appreciation to my sister, Pat for her friendship and her assistance with my initial preparation of my manuscript for publication, as well as her husband David and my friend Patti.

I wish to convey my deepest appreciation for the help and kindness of Doctors Melvin Morse and Kenneth Ring, who encouraged me to begin a chapter of the Friends of IANDS (International Association for Near-Death Studies, Inc.). Without the assistance of IANDS, the research and stories of near-death experiencers would most likely be inadequately preserved for researchers. I owe them my gratitude.

A well deserved, special thanks goes also to Meredith Young-Sowers, Publisher, Claire Gerus, Editor-in-Chief and Nancy Hanley, Staff Assistant at Stillpoint Publishing for their support of this project.

Finally, I wish to honor all my students. They have taught me much over the years; without them the world would be a shallow place, and because of them, there is more Love and Light to go around.

ANYONE
CAN SEE THE
LIGHT

Part I

It Happened To Me

1

A Glimpse of the Beyond

I WAS TWENTY-EIGHT YEARS OLD WHEN I DIED. By day I was working as an office manager for a large construction company; by night I was playing professional clarinet for several local orchestras. I loved classical music—in fact, it was my whole life, the only thing that really mattered to me.

I'd grown up in a loving family, and had enjoyed a pleasant childhood. As I'd been raised as a devout Roman Catholic, I didn't believe anyone could actually die and return to life. Now, I stand as living proof to myself, as well as to others, that one can journey to the Other Side and return.

My near-death experience occurred on a clear June morning eighteen years ago. I was preparing to give a party

17

and had been listening to a TV program while setting my hair. Penny and Tuffy, my mixed-breed pups, came bounding into the den with that "begging-for-a-treat" look, so I went to the kitchen and took a few dog biscuits from the box while the hungry pair waited eagerly, their eyes urging me to hurry.

Tuffy, who usually consumed every scrap, left a few crumbs on the floor this time. *Hmm,* I thought, *this might be a good time to clean the kitchen floor.* I went to the garage to get the mop.

While there, I noticed that the lid of the washing machine was open. "Darn," I muttered, realizing with irritation that I'd left the sheets in the machine from the previous night. Now, they smelled musty and sour from the heat of the summer day, and I knew I'd have to wash them all over again. I leaned over to remove the sheets from the machine.

Just then, the phone began to ring, so I hurriedly tossed the sheets into the laundry basket, grabbed the mop and waxer, and raced from the garage to the kitchen. It was my friend Tammy calling to see how my party preparations were coming along. We talked briefly, then said goodbye so I wouldn't end up greeting my guests with a head full of curlers.

Grabbing the mop, I dipped it into hot water and started on the kitchen floor. The minutes ticked by, and after awhile I realized that I wanted to stop this tedious chore. But I told myself, "Keep going, keep going." As I made progress, I was relieved to see that the floor was looking a lot cleaner. Not that it was perfect, but I knew that my desire for perfection was hard to satisfy. I had always been so judgmental of everything and everybody, especially myself.

Finally, I was finished. As I walked through the den, I noticed with surprise that a large wet spot seemed to be spreading beneath my fish tank. I had cleaned the tank earlier, but now two square feet of carpet beneath it were soaking wet. My aquarium is unusual in that it hangs on the wall like a framed picture. As I looked up at it, alarmed, I saw that it was nearly empty. Relieved, I now recalled that its inhabitants—several guppies—were still in the spare tank in the kitchen, waiting to be returned to the main tank. As I ran to get a towel, I consoled them, "Be glad you're in here, because your boat is sinking! But don't worry, in no time at all I'll have everything back to normal."

When I examined the tank, I quickly discovered the problem. The plastic tubing was siphoning water from the tank and spurting it out like a garden hose.

I'd done some minor wiring in the past and had always had a healthy respect for electricity, but I didn't consider it necessary to turn the power off to fix the fish tank tubing. After all, only air flowed through the tubing, not electric current. What I didn't know at the time was that the pump had malfunctioned and was now pumping electric current, not air, through the water!

I bent over to pick up the plastic tubing. As I began to straighten up, I accidentally bumped the tubing on the edge of the tank. The water suddenly squirted across my face—the pain was so sharp, it felt as if a knife were slitting my cheek! I screamed from the shock and pain, then felt a moment of temporary relief as the water crossed over my molars. My reprieve was short-lived, however, as the electrified water rushed into my mouth.

The defective pump, the metal bobby pins in my wet hair, the wet carpet on the slab floor all combined to set the stage for my electrocution.

As my body bent over in shock, I had the most uncanny knowledge that death was ahead of me. I began to mourn the loss of everything I'd known: the Earth, my home, my friends—all that I'd been aware of, all that I loved. Everything I'd believed to be true and lasting was slipping away from me. I was face to face with death, face to face with the unknown.

Against my will, my arms and legs went limp. I fought to stay alive, but an all-consuming fatigue swept through my body. As I struggled to hold onto life, I wondered, *What's going to happen to me? What should I do? How can I stop this?* But it was too late; my body was already giving in to Death's urgings.

Then came my very last conscious thought. As I looked for the last time at the fish tank and at the tubing still in my hand, I realized, *I should not have touched it.*

My body was thrown backwards and to one side by the current. As it fell, it bumped a philodendron in a hanging pot, which began to sway back and forth. My body crashed to the floor, thrown with such force that my head went right through the drywall, about a foot above the floor. I never felt the injuries, however, because I was no longer in my body. I was actually watching my electrocution from above!

I learned later that, when electrified water enters the body through a mucous membrane, it goes directly to the heart and stops it. I was unconscious even before I began to fall, but my spirit, the part of me that was out of my body, remained aware, retaining all conscious knowledge of the person known as "Dianne," and the details of her life.

How could I be out of my body and still be alive? I wondered, astonished.

Suddenly, I was aware that I was inside a vast, seemingly infinite blackness. I wasn't sure where it was, but for some reason I was unafraid. Apparently, this blackout period often occurs in near-death experiences. According to researcher Robert Crookall, if the period of time is very brief, the blackness can pass unnoticed; if it is lengthy, a person can feel as if he or she is going through a dark tunnel.

My blackout period was brief, for I now found myself back in my home, but in a new form. I was transparent, yet I still looked like me. I could see my surroundings and my spirit body vividly, as the philodendron still swayed back and forth beside me.

How elated I felt! Now, out of my body, I had no worries, no cares. Never had I felt like this when I was "alive."

It seemed as if I had moved out of my lifeless body effortlessly, and naturally. In fact, the shock of 119 volts of electricity had forced me out.

I floated to the floor. Looking down, I saw that I had legs, but somehow, I could see through them. In fact, I could see through all of me—my hands, my feet, my body, everything. My entire spirit body was transparent, and I was inside a glowing white light that extended about three feet around me.

I also saw how I looked from outside my spirit body. I seemed to be wrapped or clothed in some kind of cheese-cloth-like fabric.

Suddenly, I realized I could see perfectly without my glasses, which had fallen off and were on the floor under the fish tank. Since I'd always been extremely nearsighted, I was stunned that I could see in such fine detail. Later, when I read *Life After Life* by Dr. Raymond Moody, I learned that my experience was quite common.

"People who die may find themselves looking upon their own physical bodies from a point outside of it, as though they were spectators, or watching figures and events on a stage," says Dr. Moody.

As I floated above my physical body lifeless and unaware, I wondered, *Can I save her?* Yet, I felt no urge to act.

I looked down and knew that the body below me was a previous part of myself. *Will it awaken?* I wondered. I wanted to touch my lifeless body, wondering if a touch would rouse it. But I hesitated to do so because I feared I might be saying farewell to it.

At that moment, an awareness overtook me—I am not my physical body! This realization made me feel so free, so wonderful! My spirit was glowing with a white light that illuminated the entire room. I tilted my head and looked down at my body once again, this time with a sense of compassion. I had no tears for Dianne, no remorse. My spirit was free!

Then, I was up near the ceiling again. Everything still looked the same—the furnishings, the walls—but there was a new dimension to the scene—it had become transparent. I could see everything more clearly than ever before, and like a scientist, I found myself looking at life through a microscope, discovering minuscule particles of matter normally invisible.

My spirit was still glowing and so was the room. Seeing with my "spirit eyes" was like looking through a very delicate piece of white chiffon. Now I realized that, although my spirit body was in the den, I could see through the walls to the phone in the kitchen.

Suddenly, I had a strong urge to call for help; I wanted to save Dianne. My spirit body walked quickly through both hallway walls to the phone and I tried to pick up the receiver, but my spirit hand went right through it. Fascinated, I studied my hand carefully, looking for a cut. To my amazement, I realized I was looking right through it.

I was now aware of the absence of physical sensations, yet I was feeling a heightened sense of awareness such as I'd never felt while alive. I knew I was different from the "Dianne" I had been, but I also knew I was "me." It was similar to looking at your reflection in a mirror; you know you're not the reflection, but it does appear to be you.

Now, I saw that everything was shrouded by a mist. Despite a lack of gravity, I could easily control my direction, and when I moved into the living room, noticed that I had just walked through the glass coffee table. *Wow! How did I do that?* I marveled. I experimented with my right leg, moving it back and forth through the table, even through the beveled edge. It was effortless and quite thrilling!

Soon, I found myself going back to the den, where I began floating up toward the ceiling again. Looking down, I saw how my physical form had been thrown by the electric shock. My body was lying on its stomach, head turned to the right, knees bent slightly to one side. My left arm was under my stomach, and my right arm was bent at the elbow. My right hand was slightly open, palm down on the rug.

Tuffy suddenly entered the den and began nipping at my face and pawing at my arm, trying to get my body to wake up. I knew that his relentless attempts to awaken my physical body wouldn't work, yet I was proud of him for trying, and even hoped his efforts might work. Although his attempts did fail, he persisted. Still floating on the ceiling I thought, *Good boy, good boy.*

I wondered where his chum, Penny, was, and suddenly I was next to her in the backyard. I opened my mouth to talk to her and felt my tongue moving, but no sounds came out. I could distinctly hear my voice, and then realized it was coming from my mind. I tried several times to get Penny's attention, yelling, "Penny, can you see me? Penny, can you hear me?" Apparently she didn't, because there was no response.

Next, I walked around my backyard. As I looked through the walls of my house toward the front sidewalk, I noticed a man walking down the street. Eagerly, I flew to him, right through the walls, and tried to get his attention. Staring deeply into his eyes, I said forcefully, "Can you help me? I need help." Then I tried to shake his shoulders, but he still didn't notice me. Frustrated, I tried to touch his shoulder to get him to look at me, and my hand went through his upper right shoulder blade and out his back. This startled me. Dr. Moody was one of the first to discover that those in spirit form are invisible, as well as inaudible, to people still in their bodies.

What am I to do? I wondered, becoming upset when I realized that the man could neither see nor hear me. Instantly, I was back in my yard again, Penny beside me. I noticed that whenever I felt any apprehension, I was instantly moved to a place of greater comfort.

I walked onto my backyard patio, and to my surprise found that the pebbles in the concrete weren't hurting my bare feet as they had when I was in physical form. My feet had always been sensitive. In fact, as a little girl, I had been tormented by arthritic spurs on them, and despite several operations, had found walking to be frequently painful. I'd never dreamed that I could one day walk without pain. Yet, as I looked down to see why my feet were not hurting, I could hardly believe what I saw. I was floating about eight inches off the ground!

I decided to go back into the house, but couldn't open the sliding glass door with my hand because it went right through the solid handle. *I'd better lean back and give the door a really hard push*, I decided. But as soon as I formed the thought, I found myself gliding right through the plate glass window. I can only compare this experience to the sensation of moving your hand through the top layer of very still water in a basin. As I was passing through the window, I heard a "whooshing" sound in my head, and at that moment, I knew I'd walked through glass before. But I'd never left my body before—had I?

On the way back to the den, I stopped right in the middle of the wall between rooms. I sensed that I was to look down at something fantastic, and as I gazed downward, I saw a long silver cord coming out of my spirit body, right through the cheesecloth-like fabric I was wearing. The cord extended down and out in front of me, and as I turned around, I saw that the silver cord draped around and behind me, like an umbilical cord. I followed it through the two hallway walls and into my den, where I saw it attached to the back of the head of my physical body. The cord was about an inch wide and sparkled like Christmas tree tinsel!

Researchers studying near-death experiences believe that the silver cord is a temporarily extended linkage between the conscious spirit and the vacated body. The cord is mentioned as far back as in *Ecclesiastes 8: 6-7*: "Remember your Creator . . . before the silver cord is loosed, or the golden bowl is broken, or the pitcher shattered at the fountain, or the wheel broken at the well. Then the dust will return to the Earth as it was, and the spirit will return to God who gave it."

As soon as I saw that the silver cord was attached to my physical body, my spirit body was thrust into a dark tunnel. I moved through it with great speed, traveling faster than I could have imagined possible. Although the tunnel was filled with an all consuming darkness, I felt peaceful and unafraid. Other travelers have described the tunnel as "another dimension," "a cave," "a well," "a trough," "an enclosure," "a funnel," "a vacuum," "an emptiness," "a blackness," "a valley," or "a cylinder."

When I came to the end of the darkness, I stepped into a new dimension. Here, I could sense the presence of a loving spirit, sent—I knew—by God to greet me. Then, I was back at the site of my physical body. Back and forth I traveled through the tunnel, several times in succession, moving from the Other Side to my electrocuted physical body and back again.

Each time I emerged from the tunnel, I was met by a radiant angelic being who stood before me, smiling. The being had no wings, and I sensed it was female. She was everything I'd ever dreamed an angel would be. As she moved toward me, I walked to meet her. Her love surrounded me, and my spirit was filled with an almost unbearable joy. The love this angelic being radiated towards me made me feel that she cared more about me than anyone else ever had or could. Her love filled every particle of my being, every thought, and every emotion within me. I felt completely comforted and reassured.

She "spoke" by sending words directly into my mind. *How can I hear her thoughts before she utters them*, I wondered. Yet, at the same time I was hearing her questions, I was answering them! This marvelous being seemed to know all my thoughts instantly, just as I immediately knew hers. Although I was standing directly before her, I could see her from every angle: front, back, top, bottom, and both sides—like a cubist painting by Picasso.

She walked closer and stood with me; then, we were both lifted about ten inches into the air, as if we were on a platform moving upward. Extending her arm before her, she indicated that I was to look to my left. I did so, my heart and soul completely open to her, for I knew God had sent her to help me decide what I should do with my physical body.

As I turned my eyes left, the entire scene changed into a Life Review, a vivid, three-dimensional color display of my entire life. Every detail of every second, every feeling, every thought while I had been alive on Earth was displayed before me in perfect chronological order, from my birth until my electrocution.

At the same time, to my amazement, I was re-living my entire twenty-eight years simultaneously! The best experiences brought me feelings of great joy, as if God were talking to me through the angelic being, sharing the highest moments of my life. I felt as if every spirit in Heaven was watching with me, applauding me and letting me know that God approved of my caring, unselfish deeds. It was then that I asked myself, *Am I dead? Am I really dead?*

As the Life Review continued, I was shown two very special deeds I had performed. As these scenes were displayed before me, every emotion I had originally felt returned in full force. I also felt as if God and the angelic being were honoring me for having performed those deeds.

I will never forget the love that surrounded me at that moment, or the joy that ran through me. Can you imagine being hugged by God and your angel? It's an experience that defies description!

The first deed I witnessed had occurred the day I stopped my car to help push a woman's stalled station wagon out of mainstream traffic and into a supermarket driveway. The driver had been struggling to push the car by herself, and I felt compelled to give her a helping hand.

After I had helped push her vehicle to safety, I rushed back to my car, afraid of getting a ticket for being double-parked. In my haste, I hadn't given her a chance to thank me. While reviewing this scene, I was filled with indescribable feelings of love, which seemed to be directed to me from angelic beings high above me.

Then, my angel showed me a second vision, a scene I'd forgotten. I now saw myself at seventeen, when I'd worked at a convalescent hospital after school. I had grown fond of a toothless old woman who was no longer able to speak clearly, and who never had visitors. She liked to suck on graham crackers before going to bed, but no one wanted to serve her because when she had finished, she would drool as she kissed the entire length of the arm of the person feeding her. While others avoided her, I willingly fed her the cookies she adored, seeing how happy this made her.

When that scene was replayed for me, I felt as if every loving spirit in God's kingdom was thanking me in unison. I was amazed that such an act could have meant so much to God—and to me. I felt humbled and very honored.

A glow surrounded the radiant being as she presented my Life Review, continuing to communicate with me telepathically. As I viewed the scenes of my life, it felt as if I were absorbing many books all at once with perfect clarity.

Finally, my Life Review was finished, and I was whisked away from the angelic being and returned to the tunnel. This time, I seemed to be falling through it, finally emerging in another room, in another dimension. It was a world far more beautiful than any I could ever have imagined, a place of awesome serenity. The peace and calm I felt surpassed any previous notions I had had about Heaven, and I knew, in the deepest part of my soul, that God was here.

In this rapturous place, I recognized that there were two aspects of "me." My soul was my consciousness, everything that had made me who I had been and what I had become. My spirit, on the other hand, was the part of me that was now transparent and glowing, dressed in white.

As I looked around me, I initially found everything dimly lit. Then, I clearly saw a canopy bed resting in the center of an infinite vista stretched out before me. The bed was actually glowing within a Heavenly radiance which enveloped me as well.

To my astonishment, I saw a duplicate of myself lying on the bed. *How can there be two of me? Or three of me?* I wondered. But I was instantly reassured by the loving vibrations around me. The feeling reminded me of being reassured by a dear, trusted friend saying, "Don't worry, all is well."

There were two things I knew for certain: first, that I was Dianne, and second, that my physical body was dead. I also knew that the duplicate of Dianne on the bed was another me, but I did not know what she represented. Now, I was beginning to feel as if I were in three places at once!

One part of me was the transparent Dianne on the bed. The second was my physical body in the den, the body that no longer had life. The third part of me was my spirit, now out of its body. This part of me remained conscious and aware of all my experiences, both here and back on Earth.

I knew beyond a doubt that I wanted to stay in this magnificent place, where I felt so loved, so accepted. How does one feel "accepted" by a place? Let me put it this way: as I walked toward the bed, I could actually "feel" Heaven all around me. The rapture and peace were beyond my wildest imaginings, and I wanted to stay here forever and ever.

Do you remember how it felt, long ago, to be held and rocked in your mother's loving arms? Take this to the hundredth power and you're still light-years away from the feeling of total peace and comfort that surrounded me. I felt the love of every mother in the universe being poured inside me for now and for all eternity.

Although the bed before me was not my bed, the sheets looked amazingly like my own. I could hardly believe it when I realized that they were actually breathing, filled with life! The canopy bed was also alive, not made of the dense physical matter it would have been created from on Earth.

As I walked closer to the bed, it radiated such love to me that I knew no earthly painter or craftsman could have created it—not Leonardo da Vinci, not Rembrandt, not Michelangelo, not Monet. This bed had been made by God.

A canopy of lace hung over the bed, but it was not just any lace; it had been crafted by God. He had knotted every knot and tied every thread. The white, glowing threads were alive, breathing, and full of God and Light! God had made this Heavenly bed in for me, and I remember wondering, *How could something as beautiful as this be happening to me?*

Now, the Light was welcoming me, inviting me to recline on this Heavenly creation. The transparent "me" was gone, and as I lay down, I felt the lace caressing me with rapture, peace, and love. I was moved to tears of joy.

The top of the canopy reached to about fifteen feet. The bed was larger than a normal twin size, yet smaller than a double, and it was higher than any bed I had ever seen. The flowers on the sheets were also alive and breathing, and as I stared at the exquisitely intricate patterns in the lace, I could feel a life force of Love breathing all around me.

At that moment, I knew that nothing ever dies. Nothing ever dies!

I also knew that I would never die. If I stayed in this place, I knew I would be alive, but in a different way than I had been before my electrocution. I would still be Dianne, and I would still have my memories, but I would also feel this unbelievable love around me forever. How I longed to stay!

Then, I sensed that I must to look to my right, through the lace. There, I could see a pinpoint of Light coming from the next room, the next dimension, the infinity beyond. I knew I must see more clearly, so with my right hand I lifted up the lace. I knew I had no choice but to look.

The pinpoint of Light became a brilliant white beam a trillion times brighter than the brightest sun imaginable, and began to move toward me. At first, it appeared to be bands of multifaceted light being stretched and pulled together. I knew this Light was the presence of God.

I was awestruck, overwhelmed by the Light, the love, the love of God for me! I knew I could go into this Light, which was part of a tremendous force. And, although the Light was brighter than a thousand suns, it didn't hurt my eyes.

I was going to have to choose between staying in the Light and going back to Earth. Somehow, I knew that if I went into the next room, into the Light, I could never return to my body.

I felt torn between two desires: wanting to go into the Light, and wanting to touch something tangible and retain my connection with all that was physical. Both desires grew stronger. The Light became more intense, more radiant, more loving. As I lifted the lace and extended my hand toward the brilliance, wanting to touch the Light, it rushed under the lace and touched the outstretched middle finger of my right hand.

As soon as the Light touched me, I was transformed. The Light and my spirit merged—I had entered the Light of God, and all sense of my spirit body was gone. My consciousness, fully alive, was now totally connected to God.

Within the Light, I knew that everyone and everything is connected to it. God is in everyone, always and forever. Within the Light was the cure for all diseases; within the

Light was all the knowledge of every planet, every galaxy, every universe. Indeed, the Light was Wisdom and Love beyond all comprehension.

Being one with the Light was like suddenly knowing every grain of sand on every planet, in every galaxy, in every universe, and at the same time knowing why God had put every grain of sand in its particular place. The Light held within it the knowledge of every book in every language, from the beginning of creation to the end of time. The Light knew why every author had put every word exactly where it was. The Light conveyed the message that each grain of sand, each plant, rock, animal, and human being has a purpose and that nothing ever dies because after death, there is a new life on the Other Side.

This Light and my spirit mingled for what felt like an eternity, but eventually I began to sense with great urgency that the time had come to choose whether I would stay here or return to physical life. How could I decide?

Suddenly, my spirit body was back in the tunnel. Again, when I emerged from the tunnel, the angelic being was waiting for me. Now, I noticed that her hair was brown and turned under just above her heavenly shoulders. Each of her features was now more clearly visible as I paid closer attention to them. Breathing did not seem necessary for her or for me, yet we were both full of life. She looked at me and asked telepathically, "What do you want, Dianne?"

I said, "I want to go into the Light, and I want to touch things."

She asked me thousands of questions all at the same time, and I responded to them, communicating directly from my mind to hers.

Her angelic voice asked, "Have you ever felt this much love?"

I answered, "No."

"Have you ever felt this much joy?"

"No."

"Have you ever felt this much peace?"

"No."

"Have you ever felt this much rapture?"

"No."

"Have you ever experienced this much bliss?"

"No."

"Have you ever felt this much kindness?"

"No."

Thousands of questions, one within the other, one on top of another, all of the questions at once, yet separately.

I wanted desperately to go into the Light again. Then, the radiant being asked, "Are you sure, Dianne?"

"Yes," I replied. Of course I was sure!

I was suddenly thrust forward through the tunnel, and when I looked down, I was aghast to see my physical body below me. It looked dead and lifeless, but this time I was disinterested whether I saved it or not.

What mattered to me was the Light. I wanted the Light. I was again thrust forward through the tunnel. The angelic being was still there, waiting for me to truly decide about my life, waiting for me to decide about death, waiting for me to decide about my future.

This time she was even more radiant, more loving. I had never imagined feeling such bliss, and I felt boundless love for her. She asked, "Have you ever been in a world without pain?"

I answered, "No."

She asked, "Have you ever been in a world without war?"

I answered, "No."

"Have you ever been in a world without anger, without rage, without grief, without sadness, without envy, without poverty, without jealousy, without worry, without tears?" Again, thousands of questions, all at the same time.

I answered them all the same way—emphatically, "No." I knew that no other place in the universe could feel as good, as loving, as peaceful as this Heavenly place.

For some reason, however, the angelic being sent me into the tunnel again, back and forth through many tunnels. I wondered why. I still wanted to "touch," but I wanted the Light—both desires tugging at my spirit.

I finally found myself back in my house, once again looking down at my physical body. This time, I realized that my physical body had the potential to live again. I had begun to care less and less whether I returned to my physical body, but at this moment, looking down at my body, my attitude underwent a change. I thought, *How sad; she has done so very little.* I realized "Dianne" hadn't touched as many people as she could have while alive. And I realized how life could be enriched by touching other lives more deeply and meaningfully.

While alive, as Dianne, I had always known that my life was full of certain pleasures: a beautiful home, a good job, a nice car, warm friends, a wonderful family, a beloved best friend, and a musical career I loved. *But none of these matter any more,* I thought, reversing myself again. Only the Light mattered. Only God mattered.

To my surprise, I began to feel a persistent pulling sensation from about four inches above my navel. I tried to resist it, for I sensed a new process was beginning, one that might take me from this place, from God. I didn't want to leave behind such feelings of elation. Yes, I wanted to touch things, but I wanted the Light even more.

Suddenly, I was rushing through the tunnel again. When I emerged, I was up near the ceiling in the den, looking down at my physical body below me. Then, without warning, I was thrust swiftly back into my body, entering through the back of my neck, with my spirit legs and arms together, like a diver doing a jackknife.

As I re-entered my body, I knew that the God within me could never die, and I knew that I could never die.

Tentatively, I opened my eyes. I could still see through the hallway wall to the room on the other side where Tuffy was running from me, his little paws skidding across the waxed kitchen floor. I guessed that my awakening must have scared him, and I regretted having frightened him.

For a moment, I actually saw myself half in and half out of my body. Then, with a jolt, I landed fully back in my body.

Where was I? I was totally perplexed by my new surroundings. My mind slowly began to slip into gear again. I could feel the shag rug under the fingertips of my right hand, and I knew that my hand was no longer touching the flowered sheets on God's Heavenly bed. Instead, I was back in my physical body. Instantly, I was aware that I had been dead, and I knew that I wanted to go right back into the Light.

Oh, my God, I thought, *How could I have chosen to come back? I want to be in the Light again.* Tears ran down my cheeks and I wept, desolate about the choice that had been made. Had it really been my choice? I couldn't believe that I had decided to come back. Later, I learned that virtually all near-death experiencers report that they decided to come back or were sent back—sometimes against their wishes.

I now believe that one reason I was sent back was to help people feel better about dying—and to learn that death is not an end, but a new beginning.

Meanwhile, during the time I'd spent on the Other Side, my hair had nearly dried. Later, I could hardly believe that my amazing journey had taken less than an hour; it seemed as if I'd been gone forever.

Summoning up all my strength, I crawled to the phone and called 911. Within twenty minutes, the paramedics had arrived. They were amazed that I had awakened at all. While one paramedic attended to me, the other called the local hospital. The emergency room doctor warned him that there might be complications from the electric shock, perhaps even brain damage, since the electric current had entered my mouth.

Alternating current, I learned, is from three to five times more dangerous than direct current. Doctors later told me that even a small amount of alternating current traveling through the chest for just a fraction of a second will stop the heart. My case was even more serious, as water had been introduced into my mucous membranes, lowering my body's resistance to electric current.

When the paramedics found me, my skin was wet to the touch; perspiration had been created by the heat generated when the electric current passed through my body's tissues. I also had a knot on the back of my head where I had hit the wall when my body was thrown nearly seven feet. My pulse was still abnormally slow, so the medic insisted I be taken to the hospital.

Later, as I lay on the gurney in the emergency room, I felt totally miserable. My skin was still clammy and I had an intense headache right inside my eyes. The doctor took one look at me and ordered a complete skull series, an electrocardiogram, and blood work. The diagnosis was electric shock with heart arrhythmia (which persisted for many hours); excessive perspiration due to electric shock; postconcussive syndrome causing severe nausea, and a persistent headache. I had been unconscious for at least thirty-five minutes, and I was bruised. Fortunately, there was no skull fracture.

The examining doctor told me that miracles do happen. I seemed to have experienced one of them. Given the kind of electric shock I had undergone, my heart could indeed have stopped permanently. Considering the voltage I had received, I was very lucky to be alive.

While I was in the emergency room, one doctor after another picked up my chart and asked me questions like, "What's your name?" and "How do you feel?" I kept assuring them that I felt all right and that I just wanted to go back home. Hours passed. I closed my eyes but could not sleep. How could I, after my life-changing experience? All I could think about was the radiant angelic being, the tunnel I had gone through innumerable times to get to her, and the incredible amount of Love that existed in the Light.

Suddenly, a great sense of loneliness came over me as I remembered how it had felt to be in a place of such serenity. I remembered the loving canopy bed, and how I had found God. My eyes again filled with tears. I wanted to go back into the Light. I wanted to be with God again.

A neurologist approached me in the emergency room. My heart was still being monitored, and as he examined the tape from the electrocardiograph machine, he asked, "How do you feel now?"

41

"Fine," I answered vaguely. My mind was still reliving my conversations with the radiant being, and I knew she loved me more than anyone could be loved on Earth.

"Are you sure you feel okay?" he insisted.

"Certainly," I replied, beginning to feel annoyed. "Why?" I wanted him to leave me alone so I could go back to recalling every detail from my visit to the Other Side.

He picked up my foot and asked, "Can you feel this?"

"Yes," I said, thinking how odd these tests were.

Another doctor came in and began to question me further. "I understand from the paramedics that you were dead for a time. Did you see yourself from above?"

"Yes," I admitted, surprised at his question. I wondered how he knew I'd been up near the ceiling. Certainly, I hadn't told anyone about that part of my electrocution, but others who had "died" and been taken to that hospital had evidently reported similar experiences.

"You know you're very lucky to be here, don't you?" the new doctor added.

"For sure," I said. It was hardly the way I felt, but I had no intention of telling him that I wished I were still dead.

A priest walked in from behind the curtain around my hospital gurney, and solemnly declared, "I'm concerned about you."

I was afraid he might be preparing to give me the last rites. To reassure him that I didn't need them, I said, "No, I'm okay, I'm fine, I feel wonderful." He then asked if he could bless me, and when I said "Yes," he raised his right hand in blessing.

But I was not fine. I wanted to go back to the Light. I was no longer afraid of death; in fact, I knew that death was fantastic, death was wonderful, death was radiant and peaceful. Now, I wanted to be with God again.

I closed my eyes, and felt a great sense of peace sweep over me, telling me that God was still with me, still inside me—inside everybody and everything animate and inanimate. I knew this as absolute Truth. God was part of me and everyone else, and knowing this made me feel less lonely, even though I still wanted to go back into the Light and be with Him again.

The first doctor walked in again and I asked him, "How do you think I was able to wake up?"

He smiled, shrugging his shoulders. "I don't know. Maybe it was your dog."

I said nothing, but I knew he was wrong. Tuffy hadn't awakened me. Evidently, God had sent me back, giving me a second chance at life. How special I felt to have been given a another chance to live, to hope, to love. My tears subsided, but the tears in my heart for the Light I could no longer see continued to flow.

Before I left the hospital, the doctor explained that the medical staff couldn't be sure whether or not there would be after-effects of the electrocution. They suggested that I have someone stay with me for a while.

I asked my Mom to take me straight home, so I could see exactly where God had pulled me into His Light. I needed to put together the pieces and figure out how and why it had all happened. In the car, Mom and I talked as she drove me home. She kept looking at me strangely, and finally asked me, "What happened?"

"I died," I told her. She seemed frightened by the idea, but I suppose all mothers would have had the same reaction. Mom again asked what had happened.

I tried to explain it as simply as possible. "One "me" was outside of the other "me," and the two "me's were hooked together by a silver cord." I replied honestly. To my dismay, she glared at me.

"Don't ever say that again!" she exclaimed. I knew my words had shocked her, challenging all her beliefs. I also knew our family would never have imagined an experience such as mine was possible. But it *was* possible. I *had* died and come back!

When Mom pulled into my driveway, I could hardly wait to get inside. My dogs ran up to greet me and I gave Tuffy an extra big hug.

When I walked into the living room, I found the plastic tubing still hanging from the fish tank. The floor was still a little damp, but the paramedics had put a bucket under the tank to catch the water dripping from the tube. The guppies were still alive, swimming in their extra tank on the kitchen counter. Everything was the same; everything except me. I would never be the same again.

I had been humbled by what I had learned on the Other Side: that there is no time, that no one ever dies, that all of us are joined together, that God is inside everything and all of us. The Light had already changed me. It had changed my feelings about my life, and about the world around me. Now, I was eager to live Part Two of my life!

2

Coming Back

AFTER MY NEAR-DEATH EXPERIENCE, odd things began to happen to me. On my return from the hospital, I went into the garage and discovered that the sheets were no longer in the laundry basket where I had left them, nor had they been placed elsewhere. They were gone. I suddenly realized that they were the same sheets that had been on the canopy bed when I was in the Light. But how could that be?

Some time later, I shared that realization with my sister, Pat. Softly, she asked me, "Do you think you'll see them the next time you die?" I was unsure, but I now believe that my sheets must somehow have crossed from this dimension to the Other Side. Of course, I have no proof, but I can come to no other conclusion; I cannot imagine that anyone would have stolen them. My sister later reminded me that when I was younger, I used to joke with her, saying "When this gig is over, I hope I get some rest." Never in my wildest dreams did I think I'd see a bed when I died!

My near-death experience changed me so much that I no longer wanted the same things out of life. Now, I saw the whole world differently. I knew that each person has a purpose, and so does the world as a whole. I felt unique, and every day wondered how I could use that uniqueness for the highest good for the rest of my life. Most profoundly, I wondered how I, as just one person, could change the world. It frightened me even to consider having the guts or stamina to influence other people's lives.

When I began to lecture to groups interested in near-death experiences, I received many wonderful letters about how, after hearing me speak, people's lives changed for the better. Now, they felt closer to God and were beginning to think about their purpose in life, inspiring them to look inside and see what they could do to make their dreams a reality.

Before my near-death experience, I had always thought I knew everything. Afterwards, I realized I knew nothing compared to what was known in the Light.

Surprisingly, I also discovered that I no longer liked the way I felt when I listened to an orchestra playing classical music. I realized that I had always judged music critically, waiting for a performer to make a mistake. This negative attitude began to turn my stomach as I realized how judgmental I had been about everything and everyone. I had always tried to change things and people to be the way I believed they should be.

I learned from being in the Light that if I continued to judge others as I had been doing, I would become senile before I died again! The Light of God told me that senility was created for those who would have a hard time accepting the reality of Heaven, once they had crossed over. So they are made childlike, and thus able to accept Heaven as it is.

Many people have told me that their senile friends or relatives, while alive, had indeed thought they were always right. The prospect of senility was certainly a compelling incentive to be more loving, more understanding, and less judgmental of others!

Immediately after I returned from the Other Side, I was embarrassed to tell others how judgmental I had been before my near-death experience. It took years for me to be comfortable enough to share this. But the Light changed me; afterwards, I became truly willing to look at both sides of each and every issue.

Unfortunately, blame and condemnation are pervasive on Earth. Many groups, including religions, sit in judgment of others. Since all of humanity cannot be born in the same place or under the same conditions, we have a variety of religious beliefs. The division among them is truly sad, for

49

spirituality implies loving others and learning to live together in peace.

My experience also gave me a new understanding of Heaven. My sister, Pat, and I were raised in a very religious environment. When I was nineteen years old I had even thought about becoming a nun. However, what I had been taught about death bore little resemblance to what had actually happened to me when I died. I had been told that when people died, they would either enter Heaven, or go to Hell, Limbo or Purgatory to do penance for sins they had committed while alive.

As a child, I had prayed frequently to be good enough to get into Heaven. I knew I was far from perfect, so I believed that I would have to go to Purgatory, and knew I wouldn't go to Limbo since I had been baptized. Imagine my shock when I awakened from my near-death experience knowing I had just visited Heaven!

Catholicism teaches us that Limbo is a peaceful place, but one where God would never be seen. This idea had always dismayed me, for I couldn't understand why an innocent child who had died before baptism would never see God. When I was in the Light, I learned that these children, baptized or not, would be taken to God. Everyone is accepted into His loving realm.

I also learned that every word spoken has a major effect on our planet. Because we are all connected, the vibrations go forth to affect the speaker, the person being addressed, and everyone else. Now I'm much more careful about the words I use. Although I still make mistakes, I consider what I'm going to say ahead of time. People have no idea how much they affect everything around them on a molecular level.

My near-death experience changed other things about me, too. I had developed a new talent: now, I began to leave my body almost every night while I slept. Leaving my body while asleep wasn't quite the same as being dead, but it still felt wonderful! Sometimes during my spirit flights, I could feel God again and see His Light.

Although my childhood had been filled with church duties, I had never previously dreamed of seeing Jesus. Yet, after my near-death experience, I occasionally did see Jesus during dreams and out-of-body experiences. Sometimes He told me that someone I knew would be moving on to join Him on the Other Side. And, invariably, they did.

My near-death experience also taught me that we can heal ourselves with the Light. I had always thought my feet would hurt for the rest of my life. But I was astonished when I discovered, on the Other Side, that the arthritic spurs on my feet were no longer painful. Once I had returned to my body, they began to improve.

Not long after my near-death experience, I helped my sister, Pat, get rid of a headache. Pat told the story to a television producer:

> I remember once when we were sitting in the airport, waiting for our plane to arrive. We were going to a family reunion back East. I told Dianne I had a horrible headache that had lasted all morning, no matter

what I'd done to try to get rid of it. She told me to close my eyes, and she would try to get rid of the pain.

I thought, *This is ridiculous,* but I closed my eyes and waited. Dianne said that the light around my head looked different, and saw that the pain was over my right eye. She could tell where the pain was and that annoyed me. This "new" Dianne was difficult for me to accept.

Dianne smiled and stared a little above my head. Suddenly, my headache was gone! Amazed, I asked her what she had done. She replied that she had thought about God and the Light she'd been in when she was dead, and she'd seen the Light go through her and into me. Now, I believed her.

When I heard Pat's story from off-camera, I was so moved, my eyes filled with tears. I'd had no idea that this experience had affected my sister so much.

Another healing experience was even more striking. One night, I suddenly knew that I was out of my body. I realized that I was inside a motor home I'd never seen before, but when I walked to the back of it, I saw my friend, Leah, sitting on the floor. In the driver's seat was a short man wearing a white shirt, light blue pants, and gold-rimmed glasses. The motor home looked unusual, as though it were part motor home and part school bus. It was this oddity that awakened me to the fact that I was dreaming.

I walked toward Leah and asked if she understood that she was out of her body. She said she did now that I had asked her, but wondered whether she would remember her out-of-body experience when she woke up.

I noticed she was rubbing her arm, and asked her why. She said, "I wrenched my arm yesterday, and I'm worried about it." I sat down on the floor next to her and suggested that she think of the Light and God, and let the Light heal her. "How do I do that?" she asked. I told her to imagine that the Light was all around her.

Suddenly, the bus driver veered off the road slightly, and Leah leaned sharply to her right as the bus turned and slid on the embankment. I was jolted awake.

As soon as I got up the next morning, I called Leah to see if she remembered her out-of-body experience with me. Her husband, a psychology professor, answered the telephone. I told him that I'd had an out-of-body experience with Leah, and he asked me to describe it. Leah had already shared her experience with him, and he was stunned to hear that our detailed descriptions were identical! Most impressive was the news that Leah's arm, which she had injured the previous day while diving into a pool, was completely free of pain. Such a rapid healing had seemed out of the question the day before; in fact, the injury was so severe she had told her husband she would probably have to give up her position as a lifeguard.

I continued to marvel at the many ways God had changed my life after my return from the Light. To the amazement of my friends, I stopped playing the clarinet after having performed in orchestras for ten years. I could hardly believe it myself, but I simply lost my desire to continue playing. I still loved music, but now I found myself loving what I had once loathed—elevator music! That's right—the soothing, "no-think" quality of elevator music was now far more appealing than the structured classical music I had loved all my life.

My friends never thought I would leave my job, either. I had held an excellent managerial position, but things just didn't feel the same now. I needed something else, and now felt a deep urge to help others. This was strange for me—I certainly hadn't felt these urges before I had died. Previously, I had helped others because I hoped they would like me more. Now, my newfound desire to make life better for others was based on a sincere, unselfish desire to give of myself in whatever way was needed.

I began to share my near-death experience with those close to me: first my relatives—later, others. One day, I was drawn to share my story with my housekeeper. She was intrigued, as death had always frightened her. As I described how peaceful and happy I had felt on the Other Side, she began to relax and said she felt reassured.

Two weeks later, she was murdered by her boyfriend. Although deeply upset, I was comforted by my memory of our conversation, and I knew she was no longer afraid, but was with God, happy and filled with Light.

One morning, I heard a radio interview with Dr. Thelma Moss, the former head of the Department of Parapsychology at the University of California in Los

Angeles. To my delight, she described how people often see light around both people and objects. Ever since my near-death experience, I had been seeing this strange light, so I called the radio station and made contact with Dr. Moss. She invited me to her home in the Pacific Palisades, and when we were together, questioned me about the lights, or "auras," I was seeing. I explained that I had begun to see them immediately upon my return from the Other Side. Dr. Moss told me that many people see auras or energy fields and many, like me, have even seen their silver cords while they were out of their bodies.

When Dr. Moss invited me to share my near-death experience with her class I was honored to say "yes." The day I visited her class, I knew God had indeed sent me back to help people overcome their fear of death. When I told my story to Dr. Moss's class, some of the students cried. I cried, too, knowing that I would spend the rest of my life finding ways to share my story.

Later, I quit my job and never looked back. Before my near-death experience, being self-employed would have filled me with terror. But now, I had no choice. Since I've been on my own professionally, I've grown to love planning my own time. For the past eighteen years, I've lectured about near-death and out-of-body experiences in more than twenty colleges and universities across the country.

I am grateful to Dr. Moss for starting me on my speaking career, and for introducing me to Dr. Kenneth Ring of the University of Connecticut, who suggested I begin a Friends of IANDS (International Association of Near-Death Studies) support group in California. When I speak to groups, I always hope those who hear my story will become more open and willing to share their own near-death and out-of-body experiences.

I've found that people who hear about my journey to the Other Side are both fascinated and cautiously optimistic that a similar experience awaits them. All I can say is, once you have seen the Light and returned, life will never be the same again.

Part II

Two Doorways To Eternity

3

On the Brink of Death:
The Near-Death Experience

Unlike other books about out-of-body experiences caused by near-death situations, this book focuses on how you, the reader, can receive the benefits of a journey to the Other Side without having to risk your life! In order to understand the phenomenon of leaving your body, let's first take a look at those who left their bodies when at death's door, and then returned to continue life on This Side. The experiences will be similar to those you may encounter during your own out-of-body journeys.

Millions of people around the world have left their bodies and returned—people of all ages, of all beliefs, and from all walks of life. These amazing journeys have been reported so frequently, the subject has been assigned its own number in the library's Dewey Decimal System: 133.9013.

"I found myself floating above my body, up near the ceiling. What happened? Was I dead?" Near-death survivors continue to ask me these questions and hundreds of others, and I respond by recalling my own and others' out-of-body experiences, gleaned from years of research since I returned from Death's doorway.

As I described in Part One, after being electrocuted I was unconscious for about thirty-five minutes, with my heart affected for twenty-five of them. There was one point when I knew without question that my physical body had died. My spirit, however, was very much alive. This extraordinary experience changed my life: it altered my beliefs, my attitudes, my desire to learn, my judgment of others, my intuitive abilities, my spirituality, my concept of time and space, and my belief in angels. Others who have visited the Other Side report that their lives, too, have been forever changed.

Near-death experiences can occur spontaneously when an individual's physical body is close to death, due to cardiac arrest, shock, coma, surgery, unconsciousness, accidents, physical injury, arrhythmia, seizures, suicide, or severe allergic reactions. During that time, the person's spirit body leaves the physical body and may look down on the scene below.

These out-of-body experiences occur with surprising frequency. In fact, the most recent Gallup Poll on the subject revealed that eight million people in the United States alone had had a near-death experience! Another thirty-five percent of United States residents reported having had out-of-body experiences while sleeping.

Today, researchers have collected information about more than thirteen million near-death experiences! In the eighteen years I have led workshops on the subject, more than 25,000 people have attended my classes and many have shared their out-of-body adventures with me. Every one of them was fascinating.

The length of time one is "dead" seems to have little bearing on whether or not an out-of-body experience is reported. The longest recorded instance of a person being declared clinically dead, then returning to life, is seventy-two hours. The man, a medical doctor, was pronounced dead and spent three days on ice in the morgue. When he awoke, he described a profound near-death experience.

On the other hand, a woman who had stopped breathing and had no heartbeat for over twenty-four hours was given up for lost when, to the amazement of the attending medical personnel, she began moving her fingers. Afterwards, she had absolutely no recall of a near-death experience. Yet, reports from others who were clinically dead for shorter periods of time describe vivid near-death and out-of-body experiences.

We have also learned that two people can have a simultaneous near-death experience. One of my students, a middle-aged woman named Elizabeth, was traveling with her son when they were in a disastrous auto accident. As they approached death, each of them saw the Light and felt themselves being drawn close to the loving presence of God. Elizabeth asked God not to take her son, while her son asked God to spare his mother any injuries. Later, while recovering, both remembered their experiences in great detail. They also recalled that just before the accident, they had looked at each other and agreed to tighten their seat belts. This action probably saved their lives.

Statistics supporting near-death experiences are growing. Dr. Fred W. Schoonmaker, Director of Cardiovascular Services at St. Luke's hospital in Colorado, found that sixty-one percent of patients who were close to death described a near-death experience.

Here's one such encounter, told by my student, Doris, a retired probation officer who had been hospitalized for congestive heart failure.

> I was unable to breathe without a respirator. When I began to improve, the nurse unhooked the intubation equipment, and I was happy that she was removing the uncomfortable appliance. I suddenly heard a beautiful, richly modulated voice in my head. I had heard this voice once many years earlier when, after several days of labor, I had delivered a child.

Suddenly, all was calm. I felt regret for my surviving loved ones and a sense that "at last I can rest and not be in pain." Then I began to see a Light ahead. My body was to my left. I was looking forward to having the answers to many questions, and there was a strong feeling of love around me.

Since this experience, I no longer fear death.

Helen, an author and graphic artist, also had a near-death experience when her health was threatened.

During surgery for hemorrhaging and tumor removal, I received several blood transfusions. During one of these, I saw my physical body below me. I felt happy and peaceful, with no sense of time. Then, I knew I had to come back to care for a young girl who needed my help. I also knew someone was going to cut into my heart, and when a needle was jabbed into it, I felt a sharp twinge.

When I awakened, I opened my eyes and asked the nurse what day it was. I was amazed to learn that four days had passed. The experience changed my life—it led me to be aware of the God within me.

Bonnie, a hospital secretary, told me the following story:

I was riding on the back of a motorcycle when John and I hit the freeway divider. As I flew off the bike, my

first thought was, *Oh, God, I do not want to die! Please don't let me die!* Then I saw an intense, blinding, silver-white Light, and I had the most wonderful, peaceful feeling. I thought, *If this is how it feels to be dead, it really is not so bad. If I could just stop rolling over, I would be okay.* Then I stood up, thinking, *I have to see if John is okay.* I looked down and saw myself lying there. I remember thinking, *I can't leave now. I have children to take care of.* Previously, I'd had a horrible fear of dying; now, I no longer fear death.

Charlotte, a retired cosmetologist, reported her own near-death experience.

Heart failure caused my heart to stop for seven minutes. Then, I was resuscitated. It was like a movie. I saw a beautiful green lawn and flowers. A voice said, "Come back," and I heard myself saying, "I don't want to come back." Then I heard a voice saying, "Your time is not up." I knew I had more to do on Earth. That's when I awoke.

Sometimes, just before death, people see relatives who have passed on before them. Cory described her husband's experience this way:

My husband was in the last stages of ALS (amyotrophic lateral sclerosis), commonly known as Lou Gehrig's disease. He was hospitalized, and we knew he was close to death. During the preceding weeks, I had read to him every day from the writings of Elisabeth Kubler-Ross and Raymond Moody. Both authors gave countless descriptions of people who had been declared clinically dead and then awakened. Each description contained a statement about deceased relatives and friends coming for those who were dying.

The day Frank died, our son and I were both in his room. My husband was fully conscious, and his mind was clear to the very end. He and I talked about whether anyone would come for him. He had been unable to actually talk for months, but we had developed a means of communication whereby he would blink his eyes once for "no" and twice for "yes."

As his body began to fail, the nurse removed the blood pressure cuff and left the room. I asked my husband, "Have they come?" He looked at me, smiled a little, and blinked twice.

Later, as we walked out of the room, my son, who did not know I had been reading Kubler-Ross and Moody to my husband, said, "You know, Mom, I had the strangest feeling, when I was standing at Dad's bed, that I was looking at him over a lot of shoulders." I think he was.

4

Visiting the Other Side:
The Out-of-Body Experience

Not everyone will have a near-death experience, but anyone can have a guided out-of-body experience. Out-of-body journeys can occur at any time. Experiencers report having had them while jogging, dreaming, making love, praying, driving or meditating, during time of stress, excitement, fear, or physical exhaustion, and especially when sleeping.

In fact, it is during the sleep state that you can most easily explore the several "keys" to having an intentional, guided out-of-body journey. Once you have achieved this, you will be on your way to one day seeing the Light. With confidence, you can join the ministers, lawyers, physicians, engineers, priests, nuns, nurses, artists, musicians, computer analysts, pilots and others who have shared their experiences with me afterwards.

Do you recall dreams in which you're flying? Do you have vivid dreams, often in color? If so, you're probably a good candidate for an out-of-body experience while you're asleep.

One night, during a flying dream, Johannah, an artist and accountant, recognized that she was out of her body.

> I was in the air, arms spread, gliding over treetops, over an unfamiliar town. My excitement was over-whelming. All I could think was, *Wait until I tell Dianne I finally made it!* I looked toward the horizon and saw a futuristic city. It was glowing white and translucent.

I've loved working with people who want to experience guided out-of-body travel. My near-death experience occurred in 1977, before much had been written about near-death or out-of-body experiences. As more and more information became available, I read everything I could put my hands on to learn more about the subject.

At first, I had a profound desire to see if I could induce the experience, and I put myself through strenuous mind and body exercises to see whether anything might prompt a similar occurrence.

(Let me be clear on one thing: I did not want to die; I wanted to live. But I so yearned to feel again the intense love and bliss I had experienced on the Other Side.)

I tried everything from sensory deprivation techniques to experiments with mental and brain-wave theories. Then, I decided to pursue a private practice in hypno-therapy, hoping to discover a way to initiate an out-of-body experience in myself or in others who wished it.

There were many reasons I wanted to re-visit the Other Side. I knew that every out-of-body journey, whether near-death or not, can change the life of the experiencer. Both types of out-of-body experience can provide knowledge otherwise unattainable. Both can create an incredible awareness of God's love. Both can awaken the deepest sense of peace and well-being. Both can even, on occasion, bring healing and recovery.

Some out-of-body experiencers have been healed of their physical problems while in the Light. Once I met a woman who was suffering excruciating pain from a serious back injury. While sitting in agony, she decided to try to leave her body, hoping to relieve her pain. She envisioned a bright white Light surrounding her body, and suddenly saw a brilliant Light filling the entire room. She felt the powerful, healing love of God, and realized she was now out of her body. When she came back a few moments later, her back pain was gone. It never returned.

I learned many things while out of my body, first during my near-death experience and later during hundreds of intentional "journeys." Four of the most important are:

1. Out-of-body experiences can create new empathy with others, and result in a deeper sense of communion with those people who have been placed in your life for love and growth.

2. When you are out of your body, your mystical connection to the universe and to God makes you realize you really are a part of everything around you. You understand that your life has a specific purpose—a much greater one than you may have imagined.

3. Out-of-body experiences show you that there are no boundaries between the past, present, and future. All is revealed instantly, in a place without time limitations.

4. Out-of-body experiences can greatly heighten your appreciation for life. If you had been taught as a child that you were directly linked to God, times of desolation or loneliness would not lead you to consider drastic acts, such as suicide. Out-of-body experiences, powerfully and exquisitely, reveal your connection to God.

Here are some more stories involving some of my students who succeeded in having out-of-body experiences.

Peter, a member of my class, spontaneously decided to visit my home one night while out of his body. That same evening, I had a very vivid out-of-body experience in which I saw Peter standing in the doorway of my bedroom. He then approached my kitchen, putting his hand through the walls as he walked.

When Peter arrived for the next class two weeks later, I asked if he remembered seeing me in my home. He looked disconcerted, and then showed me his dream book. In it was a description of his out-of-body visit to my home. Embarrassed, he revealed that he had seen something a bit puzzling. After I encouraged him to tell us what it was, he said that he'd wondered why my husband and I were not sleeping in the same room.

I was impressed, as I'd never revealed this information to anyone in the class. I went on to explain that my husband has sleep apnea and makes a great deal of noise snoring. Therefore, we sleep in separate rooms. Peter then went on to accurately describe the entire layout of my home.

How else could this information have been obtained, other than during a very successful out-of-body visit from my curious student?

When we discuss out-of-body experiences in my classes, I tell students it's fine to inform someone that you're going to try to visit; the only drawback is that skeptics may believe the visitor is actually a product of wishful thinking. Unplanned visits are more verifiable when both parties involved write down each night's dreams and out-of-body experiences independently, and later compare them.

A computer software administrator named Deborah had an out-of-body experience after taking my class. She told me that after lying in bed for about two hours, she had decided to roll over and go to sleep. A few minutes later she "fell out of bed."

I got up thinking how lucky I was not to have hurt myself on the night table, but when I climbed back into bed I promptly fell out again. As I got up the second time I realized, with a start, that I had fallen right through the night table, and then I knew I was out of my body!

Some out-of-body experiences are more than fascinating; they can be life-saving. Enrique, a long-haul truck driver, reported a conscious out-of-body experience while on the highway. His is one of only two experiences I have heard in which people left their bodies while driving their vehicles!

Enrique suddenly saw himself sitting on the roof of his eighteen-wheeler, watching vehicles miles up the road crashing into each other. He instantly jolted back into his body and knew he should slow down immediately, even though there were still no signs of an accident up ahead. Sure enough, he came upon a major accident several miles farther on. He credits his out-of-body experience with saving his life, and possibly the lives of others.

In a similar case, my student, Mathew, was driving on the curve of a freeway off-ramp when the driver's side door opened. Mathew tried to catch the door by the armrest, but as he did so, his body was pulled part out the door. Although his foot was on the brake pedal, he couldn't apply the brakes because the momentum had pulled his body too far out of the vehicle. Nor could he close the door, as the force of the curve gave him no leverage.

Mathew knew with dread that an accident was imminent. Suddenly, he saw a transparent arm identical to his own coming out of his right arm. It turned the steering wheel to the right, saving him from an impending collision with an oncoming vehicle. Mathew's ability to see, while conscious, both his solid physical arm and its transparent duplicate as it moved the steering wheel, is highly unusual. He believes that he wouldn't have survived, if not for this partial out-of-body experience.

Of all the benefits an out-of-body or near-death experience brings, the most profound is its ability to remove one's fear of death. Travy, a soldier in combat in Vietnam, tells his story.

While fighting, my platoon of twenty-two men was called to go to an area that had been overtaken by the Vietcong. We came under enemy fire. The Vietcong retreated, and we stayed there all night, the dead and wounded all around us. At daybreak the First Lieutenant ordered a platoon roll call, but the enemy started shelling us and the trucks to our left took a direct rocket hit. The buildings were also destroyed and I could hear the sounds of rockets over me. At that moment, as I started for cover, I knew I was dead.

Then, I was caught up in an array of bright colors, where I felt there was no time or space. I was just floating in the colors. Suddenly, I was back in my body. The others around me had been killed, and I, too, would have been killed if I had not been out of my body. I now have no fear of death.

Some people encounter their deceased relatives during guided out-of-body experiences. After attending my classes, a woman who left her body while asleep saw her departed mother. The woman asked her mother where her last will and testament was, since no one, including her husband, could find it. She was surprised to hear her mother telling her telepathically that the will was in the glove compartment of her mother's car. Sure enough, the document was found there. Yet, her daughter had had no prior knowledge of its location, even when her mother was alive.

During an out-of-body trip, the spirit body of the traveler can sometimes be seen by a living witness. Dr. Charles Tart has researched out-of-body experiences and has found that many witnesses have seen people who were out of their bodies. One of these occurrences is cited by Johnny.

I felt real, but not physical. I was a spectator, but I was not dreaming. I was streaking across the surface of the ground at incredible speed. Suddenly, I was in the upper corner of a bedroom, looking down at a woman who was lying in bed, lamp on, awake. She saw me! I moved closer; she was startled, though not frightened— I was surprised at that. She curled up and let out a somewhat subdued squeal.

I saw what looked like old rags or clothing trailing off a soft but firm object, like an octopus. It was barely moving in the air. Yet, by the way the rags or tentacles were moving, it seemed to be going very fast. Suddenly, I was looking in from the hallway, both hands on the doorjamb. I woke up with a sudden jolt.

About a year later, I went on vacation back to my home town, and while visiting old friends I happened to see the same woman! She immediately started relating to me what she called "the little octopus experience." My mouth hung open as she described in detail the events of my earlier out-of-body experience.

An out-of-body experience can occur at any time. One man reported that he'd had several of them while reading novels! Suddenly, while in the midst of the story, he would find himself standing in the adjoining room's doorway looking back at his physical body while he continued to read his book. He knew that he was in two places at the same time, and he knew that he was out of his body.

Such incidents have also happened to marathon joggers who were fully awake when their out-of-body experiences occurred. In these cases, I believe the rhythm of running might cause a trance-like state that induces an out-of-body experience. Joggers frequently tell me they have seen themselves running from behind, dressed identically to their physical bodies. When they wonder how they can be in two places at the same time, suddenly, they are back in their bodies.

A fighter pilot told me that during a reconnaissance mission, he found he could see outside the aircraft. He wasn't puzzled by this until he discovered that he wasn't looking through the F4's windows, but through its walls! He later suggested that his out-of-body experience might have been triggered by extreme gravity force.

Some people find they have triggered an out-of-body experience during times of intense emotion. Annabelle, a teacher, related that when she was eleven years old and doing household chores, she suddenly escaped from her body.

> I had just taken a bag out into the garage. As I started down the steps I had very pronounced, very serious thoughts going through my mind. I said that I hated my body, that I did not want it any more, that I had not chosen it, so why must I put up with it? As a child I was a bronchial asthmatic and missed many days of school.
>
> At that very moment, I wished intensely that I could get rid of my body. Suddenly, my wish came true! I was hovering to the right of my physical body, slightly higher than my head. I felt "all together" but completely non-physical and completely alone.

Despite these examples, it is quite rare for an out-of-body experience to occur during the waking state.

Joseph, after attending one of my lectures, set out to have a conscious out-of-body experience. When he succeeded, he sent me a poem describing his experience.

Remember waking up
Seeing my Lightbody,
Light blue in color.
Floating down in a
Circular motion into
My physical body.
At that point
I awoke, sat up,
Said out loud,
Wow!
I now feel a deep purpose within me.

A few of my students have reported that their physical bodies were healed in the Light during a guided out-of-body experience. Although this is much more common during near-death experiences, I can relate some healing experiences from my students.

One woman who had ovarian cysts was told she needed to have a hysterectomy. She was still of childbearing age, however, and decided to try a healing technique I suggested. I told her to imagine breathing in Light through her nostrils as she drifted off to sleep, and to visualize having an out-of-body experience. When inhaling, she was to visualize the Light, and see it go to her ovaries, shrinking her cysts. When breathing out, she was to exhale only through her mouth, imagining that she was releasing all negative impressions about her cysts. She was to see these negative thoughts as blackness coming out of her mouth.

After about two weeks, she wrote me a wonderful letter telling me that her doctor was stunned.

"I can't believe it!" he had exclaimed. "These tumors are shrinking!" In fact, they had shrunk so much, the surgery was cancelled. Nor did the tumors return. Two years later, I saw the woman again, and she was expecting her second baby.

Incidentally, a healing exercise such as this one, acknowledging God and the Light around you, is effective if done just as you are entering sleep. It always works better if your doctor tells you exactly what is wrong—then you can visualize the problem in your body. By using visualization, you can add a healing image of Light to your medical treatment.

The mind is a very powerful tool. During sleep it can become even stronger, more creative, and more connected to God and your own spirituality. Imaging techniques coupled with the Light have often been known to create miracles.

You can use the same technique to help heal someone else during your dreams. As you fall asleep, think of the person you want to heal and imagine yourself and your loved one wrapped in healing white Light. This works only when you know that you are out-of-body, and that your mind is awake in your dream.

Hospitals are now examining the possibility of healing with the mind. Nurses in several university hospitals around the country are adopting a method of healing called "Therapeutic Touch." The nurses who perform

Therapeutic Touch visualize energy coming into their bodies, then flowing out from their hands into their patients. Medical schools have now proved that Therapeutic Touch does work for some people.

I have known ever since I died that the Light inside every human being can be used to help others. Believing you can actually aid the healing process is vital to your success. Just feel the desire to help others, believe you can do it, and then, see the Light coming into you and flowing out toward the afflicted area.

Tom, a machinist, learned how to have a guided out-of-body experience from his wife, who had attended my classes. He describes how he was healed during his first journey.

I awoke early but had started to fall asleep again when I noticed a distant white glow. I attempted to move myself toward the glow by "feeling" for the Light. Then, I was surrounded by stars. I set my mind on a journey, and all of a sudden there was a terrific force, a wind.

I remembered that my wife, Patti, was in the hospital and I felt I must visit her. I began to zoom and coast until I reached the nurse's station. I entered my wife's room, but she was asleep, so I asked a nurse on duty how she was doing. The nurse said there was nothing in her power that she could do for my wife.

I then asked the nurse if she could take a look at my ear infection. She went behind the nurse's station and produced an ear probe. She stuck it in my ear and said, "You can go home now."

Then, I looked "through my pillow" at my watch for the time, and realized I had returned to my body in bed. When I awoke, my earache was gone.

I have never been so moved by the story of an out-of-body experience as I was when I heard about Tammi, then a little girl of eleven years old. Her mother, Linda, came up to me after hearing me lecture at a local college on near-death experiences. Linda told me that Tammi kept reporting out-of-body travels while asleep at night. They were disturbing, however, because a man continued to come through a red door towards her. Linda wondered if I could help her daughter. She described her problem this way:

Tammi kept telling us that when she was asleep, a man would start chasing her, and she could not make him stop. She also had a hard time waking up. Then she started seeing her Dad, who had died seven years before.

The paramedics were at our home frequently because Tammi's fear caused her to hyperventilate, which led to seizure-like conditions. At the hospital, the staff would run tests on her and tell me they couldn't find out why this was happening to my daughter.

Often while out of body, I have come to the aid of friends who were out of body at the same time. I felt I might be able to help Tammi the next time she had problems.

I told Linda to have Tammi call out my name the next time she was out of body and felt in danger, and I would try to come to her assistance. Linda went home and told Tammi to call out, "Dianne!" if she was confronted by the mysterious man during sleep. Tammi gratefully agreed.

The next morning, the girl told her mother, "After I called out Dianne's name, a lady came to me dressed in black pants and a blue blouse with buttons and she kept her hand on the door so it wouldn't open." Tammi accurately described my hair, eyes, skin color and other specific details.

A week later, Linda brought Tammi to my home. I asked her to describe the first thing she'd seen when she had been paralyzed. She said, "A red door, and you were holding the red door closed to keep the man out."

I sat down with Tammi and told her all about my out-of-body experiences, so she would understand what was happening to her. I described a special technique I had learned to help me wake up during an out-of-body experience (See Key Three in Chapter 5). Later, Tammi said that when she used this method, her frightening experiences stopped. Once Tammi knew she could control the situation, her fears eased and she was able to get to sleep.

Some time after that, she had a vivid out-of-body experience with her deceased father during which he told her that he had died after being hit over the head. This was indeed true, though Tammi had never been told the story of her father's death. She has since had several out-of-body meetings with her father, all of them positive and reassuring.

As Ralph Waldo Emerson once said, "The only antidote for fear is knowledge." The more people learn about out-of-body experiences in general, the more effectively they can handle their own.

Part III

Anyone Can See The Light

5

The Seven Keys To
Seeing The Light

INTRODUCTION

W<small>HAT DO PEOPLE MEAN WHEN THEY SAY</small>, "I saw the Light
and it was incredible"? And what can *you* expect to see
when you finally have your own experience in the Light?

For some people, it's the thrill of seeing a deceased
relative surrounded by an aura of white or golden Light.
For others, it's the visual recognition of a second body,
one that everyone possesses but rarely, if ever, sees—made
of pure Light. And for those who are very fortunate, it's the
experience of seeing a radiant figure of Jesus or another
holy person bathed in celestial Light.

Still others might consider the Light to be enlightenment, as they discover truths during their out-of-body
experiences that will change their lives.

Of course, the Light that most people hope to see, and
indeed, the Light that is often reported by those returning
from a near-death experience, is the longed-for Light at the
end of the tunnel, that blinding, yet comforting blaze of
pure Love that enfolds and embraces every particle of one's
being.

Regardless of the form of Light you hope to see, once
you have mastered the art of leaving your body during
sleep or meditation, you have an excellent chance of
encountering one, if not all of these during your out-of-
body experiences. And, as you experience the realities of
other dimensions, you might find that your definition of
Light changes or expands. That's what happened to me. It
can happen to you, too.

The techniques that can enable you to see the Light are
simple. They might take time to learn, but they'll work if
you're persistent. In fact, thirty-four percent of my
students have succeeded in having a conscious, guided
out-of-body experience within two weeks of taking my
course, even if they had never had one before. The
percentage increases as time goes on.

In earlier chapters, I've described some of my students'
experiences to show you how they awakened their
consciousness to move out of body during their dream

state. These nocturnal explorers have used the out-of-body experience to find lost items, locate missing persons or pets, help heal their physical bodies, see deceased relatives or friends, or see the Light or an angelic being. All report having been deeply moved by their experiences.

In a survey I took of my students over the years, I documented how they were able to achieve their out-of-body experiences. Out of an initial 3,765 people surveyed, 224 had previously undergone near-death experiences. The rest had never had a conscious out-of-body experience. (See Appendices for more detail.)

With training, anyone can recognize when they are having an out-of-body experience. I have taught the techniques you are about to learn to more than 25,000 people, using a special system I designed to move them progressively through certain steps.

First, they learn how to recognize an out-of-body experience; then, they learn how to guide their own out-of-body journeys, as often as they wish. The more frequently these occur, the greater the chances of seeing the Light.

Each of the following Seven Keys can create the opportunity for you to have an experience that can bring you to the Light. There is no real order to these Keys, as any one of them can occur while you sleep. You might even experience more than one Key per sleep session. The trick is to learn what the Keys are, recognize when they are occurring, and act on them while you're asleep.

How, you'll doubtless ask, can I do this while I'm sleeping? Like any other skill, it's a matter of practice and preparation. But you can do it—remember, thousands of others have succeeded in repeatedly leaving their bodies by using these techniques.

HOW TO PREPARE FOR A GUIDED OUT-OF-BODY EXPERIENCE

Before I describe the Seven Keys, however, there are several preliminary steps you'll need to take to help you prepare for a guided, or self-directed, out-of-body experience.

• First, begin to record in a journal every dream you have. Soon, you'll begin to see themes and patterns, such as "flying dreams" or "lucid" dreams (more on these later in this chapter). These are signals that you may be out of your body.

• During the day, imagine yourself actually having an out-of-body experience while dreaming later that night. Choose the place or person you want to visit, and then visualize the desired image vividly in your mind.

• Before going to sleep or meditating, tell yourself that you will have an out-of-body experience.

• Just before actually falling asleep or meditating, see again in your mind's eye who or where you have chosen to visit while out of body. This might be a specific geographic location, a room in your home, or someone you love.

• While lying in bed, suggest to yourself that you will see your hand and/or foot while you are dreaming. Also remind yourself to notice the camera you have placed nearby when you return to your bed during your out-of-body experience.

• Tell yourself that your physical body will fall asleep, but that your mind will stay awake. This will allow you to observe any dream that begins. Or, you might remind yourself to awaken your conscious mind during your dream, even while your body remains physically asleep.

• Once you are aware that you are actually out of your body, keep your destination in the forefront of your mind and immediately go to it.

I know from my own experiences, as well as from those of thousands of others, that you can leave your body, reach your destination, and then return safely again and again. In the process, your fear of death will be replaced by a deep appreciation of the wonderful opportunities awaiting you every day you spend on Earth.

Here are the Seven Keys that can one day show you the Light.

1. The jolt
2. Vibrations
3. Sleep paralysis
4. Awakening twice
5. Lucid dreaming
6. Hands/feet/camera
7. Angels and radiant beings

Now, I'll describe these in detail, and let my students tell you what each one felt like for them.

KEY ONE: THE JOLT

The most common indicator, or Key, that an out-of-body experience is at hand is the jolt. This is a very common phenomenon and was observed by ninety-seven percent of participants in my study, or 3,652 people.

To describe the jolt more fully, let's observe Terry, who's getting ready for bed. She generally falls asleep quite easily, but once in a while finds that her body relaxes as she begins to sink into unconsciousness. Suddenly, she feels as if she's falling off the bed. This quickly brings Terry back to full consciousness.

What happened to her? Terry experienced the jolt, a sudden sense of moving or falling while lying in bed. This can happen on two specific occasions: either prior to falling asleep, when your muscles are beginning to relax, or when you are just returning from an out-of-body experience.

How can you tell the difference? If you're the person experiencing it, the jolt feels the same in both cases. If your partner sees you twitching or jerking in your sleep, you're simply experiencing the physical jolt that indicates your muscles are relaxing. Physicians call this sudden jolting of the body a "hypnagogic jerk." This is common and normal, and indicates that you're probably still in your body.

If, on the other hand, you're not seen moving during the jolt, you are probably returning from being out of your body, although you might not be consciously aware of it.

In order to recognize when you are having an out-of-body experience, you must first begin to pay attention to any jolt you experience. By recognizing when these occur, you will begin to train your mind to prepare for those that indicate that you are out of your body, and about to return to it.

Let's say you're lying in bed drifting off to sleep, and you suddenly feel a sharp jolt. Instead of tensing up because you're afraid of falling, welcome the sensation. This is the first step in preparing for an out-of-body experience via the jolt.

This training process may take time. Don't expect results right away; just relax and observe when the jolts occur. One day, you may suddenly find yourself on the ceiling or above your house, or you may meet a Light being or see a relative or friend who has passed on. If so, congratulations—you've succeeded in leaving your body!

Carmen, a government worker, saw her mother as a being of Light after experiencing the jolt.

> I was asleep in bed when I felt one, then another jolt, then several more. Later, I realized that with each one, I was actually going in and out of my body.
>
> During one of these jolts, I remained consciously out of my body. Then, I became aware of a presence in the room. It was my mother, who had passed away a year before. Today was her birthday.
>
> Suddenly, we were in a field. My mother was young again and radiant, wearing a white, flowing dress. I saw her approach a pond in the middle of the field and walk to it. When she emerged, she was perfectly dry. I said, "You're so beautiful," and went to embrace her, but she disappeared before my eyes.

Carmen then found herself at the ceiling looking down on her physical body. Almost instantly, she was back inside her body.

The next day, Carmen's father told her he had been sitting at the kitchen table, beginning to nod off, when he looked up and saw a beautiful young woman. It was his wife, glowing and radiating love. She stayed for about five seconds and began to disappear by fading from the feet up. (Incidentally, it's quite common for apparitions to appear in a younger form if they died in old age, and to return at a somewhat older age if they died as babies).

If you watch for the hypnogogic jolt just as you enter sleep, you may become aware later in the night if you feel a jolt while returning from an out-of-body journey. You may first become aware of being outside your body, seeming to fall from the air very quickly until you hit bottom, and then coming back into your physical body with a jolt. While you sense that you're falling, you might see yourself outdoors, possibly falling through the roof of your home, or you may be up near the ceiling looking down at your sleeping physical body just before re-entering it.

The sense of falling that accompanies the jolt can be unsettling at first. Dr. Calvin Hall of the University of California at Santa Cruz found that the most commonly reported unpleasant dream was that of falling.

Here are some more descriptions of how we may experience the jolt.

Paul, a minister, recalls:

While dozing, all at once I felt as if someone or something was jumping vigorously on the bed, because I was moving so much. I asked my wife whether she saw either me or the bed move. She said no.

Mary Ann, a nurse, recounts this experience:

I was lying on the sofa for a Sunday afternoon rest and dozed off. Soon I was dreaming that I was falling, when all of a sudden I felt a terrific jolt! I awoke

suddenly and commented to my husband that I had
jumped so hard I must nearly have fallen off the sofa.
My husband assured me that he had been watching me
fall asleep, and I hadn't moved at all.

About a week after my electrocution and near-death
experience, I felt both the jolt and a sense of flying. They
occurred during my first conscious out-of-body experience
at home. It all began when I lay down to take a nap while
thinking of a very close friend. Then, I fell asleep. Almost
at once, I was conscious of flying, and I soon arrived inside
his apartment! I could hardly believe I was there, but I
could see everything in his room. I took in every detail,
then found myself flying over Rosecrans and Paramount
Boulevards in Los Angeles, viewing the landscape and all
the cars below me.

Once back home, I flew through my closed bedroom
window. I was amazed to see the reflection of my spirit
body in my mirrored closet doors—it looked just like me—
but it was transparent! Instantly, I fell backwards into my
physical body with a jolt, suddenly wide awake.

Excitedly, I telephoned my friend and reported my
experience, describing his room in detail. I was as amazed
as he that my description was entirely accurate!

It took several months of journal-keeping and studying the phenomenon before I realized that the out-of-
body experience actually *precedes* the jolt. Many people
report hearing a whooshing, a buzzing, or the sound of

air rushing by their heads just as they awaken with the jolt—the sense of hitting bottom when re-entering their bodies.

KEY TWO: VIBRATIONS

Unlike the jolt, vibrations occur *before* the out-of-body experience begins. Upon leaving the body, people will sometimes feel their bodies tingling or vibrating. In most cases, the person will awaken suddenly, perhaps afraid something is rocking or moving them. Yet, upon arising, they discover that nothing else in the room is moving. *Was it my imagination?* they ask themselves.

When I lecture here in California, I joke that in this state, you can't always be sure whether you're feeling the vibrations or an earthquake! In my survey, twenty-four percent, or 903 respondents, reported feeling vibrations during sleep that were not earthquake related.

When vibrations herald out-of-body experiences, I suspect they're caused by a spontaneous acceleration of energy similar to the rising of the kundalini, the power center in the human body associated with transformation of consciousness. Here's what happened during one of my own experiences with vibrations:

> I was lying in bed, reflecting on the many ways one can have an out-of-body experience. I told myself that I was going to remember whether any of them occurred while I was falling asleep. Thus, rather than drifting off,

I was trying to prepare my subconscious to recognize any opportunities to leave my body that arose.

This particular evening, I awoke from a dream in which I felt myself vibrating. *Wow!* I thought. *These vibrations mean I have an opportunity to be out of my body!* I started to walk across the bedroom when I realized with shock that my feet were going through the floor. *Relax,* I told myself, not wanting the experience to end.

I was then aware that I was in a semi-solid state. I began moving toward the living room, but felt the urge to turn and see my physical body lying on the bed. To my surprise, it seemed smaller than its actual size. (I later learned that this often happens during out-of-body experiences. The change in size seems to be related to how you feel about staying connected to your body; if you feel free to leave it, it may appear smaller than it actually is.)

I moved into my kitchen and saw a flash of light. *Hmm,* I thought, *I didn't turn on the light switch. I wonder what caused the flash?* When I walked toward the switch on the wall, I suddenly "fell" into another dimension. Here, I was completely enveloped in Light and absolute love; it felt very close to what I had experienced during my electrocution. This time, however, I knew I was awake and out of my body, and not dead. I felt wonderful! Then I quickly fell through blackness, and, as I hit bottom, awoke.

Teri, an artist and psychology student, describes her experience with vibrations.

> I was lying on my bed, awake and relaxing. I was aware that my body was starting to feel light and tingly. The second time it happened, I saw next to my bed a woman with long, blond hair. She said, "Your teacher is not of this Earth.

Fiona, a housewife, recalls the following sensations:

> I had been sleeping and suddenly felt as if my body were vibrating and "humming." Yet I knew that my physical body was not moving, and neither was the bed.

Charles, a technical instructor, learned to control the vibrations.

> The vibration seems to start in my fingers; it's a tingling sensation, much like house current. If I want it to stop, it stops. If I want to examine it, I relax, and it becomes stronger. It leaves suddenly, with no ill effects.

Vibrations are often picked up by light sleepers, who tend to keep their minds on edge before falling asleep. Even a sound sleeper, however, can learn to become more aware of vibrations and tingling sensations.

KEY THREE: SLEEP PARALYSIS

One of the easiest ways to recognize that you are out-of-body during sleep is to understand "sleep paralysis." This is a temporary sense of being unable to move during sleep. It can be frightening at first, but your fears will ease once you understand why this is occurring.

Nine-year-old Jimmy is a good example of a child who experiences sleep paralysis, and thus hates to go to bed. After lying down, he begins to hear voices and thinks someone is in his room with him. When Jimmy tries to move his arm, he cannot. The next day he tells his mother about his upsetting experience. "It was just a dream, honey," she reassures him.

That night, Jimmy again lies in bed, nervous and on edge. Now, he's expecting something to happen, and this time he not only hears voices in his room, but hears someone walking on his bedroom floor. Suddenly, he realizes that he can't scream, he can't move, and he can't yell for his mommy. He tries to open his eyes and cannot, so again he attempts to cry out. In the morning, his mother tries to reassure her son by saying, "You just had another bad dream." No wonder Jimmy's afraid to go to sleep at night!

Jimmy's experience with paralysis is not unusual. But until he understands that paralysis indicates he is *partially out of his body*, he will continue to have difficulty with this stage of sleep.

To further clarify how and when paralysis occurs, let's go back to 1951, when Dr. Eugene Aserinsky discovered Rapid Eye Movement (REM). Medical sleep researchers now know that dreams are usually most vivid during REM sleep. However, it is also during REM sleep that the neurons at the base of the brain stop affecting the muscles. At this time, paralysis occurs during sleep.

It's interesting to learn that the electroencephalograph (EEG) pattern of a person who is awake is similar to their EEG pattern during REM sleep. This is true because the mind is much more alert during REM sleep than during other sleep states. REM sleep starts about ninety minutes after you fall asleep, and gradually becomes shorter with age. Adults spend about twenty percent of sleep time in the REM stage.

During the paralysis period of REM sleep, the dreamer becomes motionless, except for breathing. Any attempt to move, or even open the eyes, fails. The dreamer is convinced that someone will hear a call for help, but discovers that no sounds are coming forth. Crying out for help is upsetting because it simply cannot be done during paralysis.

Sleep researchers have only recently discovered that paralysis happens to everyone, every night during REM sleep. Most people sleep right through it, but some accidentally become aware that they are partly out of their bodies during this stage. *It is only during the paralysis stage that people can observe themselves half-in and half-out of their bodies.*

Beth, one of my students, offers a good example of both vibrations and paralysis as indicators of an out-of-body experience.

> I purposely lay down in bed to have an out-of-body experience. Suddenly, I felt as if I were on a roller coaster. I seemed to be rocking back and forth, and I was above the trees. From that vantage point, I saw all kinds of people. When I came back to my body, I felt extreme vibrations, but told myself, "It's okay. I know what this is."
>
> At that point, I couldn't tell if my eyes were open or closed, but I could see my spirit arm going back into my physical body as the vibrations continued. As soon as the two arms became one, the vibrations stopped . . . .

Beth's is a good example of how to use two Keys to stay connected with an out-of-body journey. First, she was awakened by vibrations. Then, she saw her spirit arm merge with her physical arm.

Sleep paralysis occurs within every age group. The respondents in my survey ranged from ages nine to seventy-eight. About eighty-five percent of them had never told anyone about their paralysis experiences, and most believed they were the only ones who had ever experienced it. Some people hear voices during paralysis, some see their rooms lit up (although the lights are actually out and their eyes are closed), some see their deceased relatives but *none of them can move until they are out of REM sleep.* Or, to put it another way, no one can move during paralysis until they are totally back in their bodies.

This is how respondents reported their inability to move during paralysis:

Cathe, an accounting secretary, said:

> After going to bed I noticed I could not move my legs and could not talk. I could feel my body behind me.

Sally, a nurse, told me:

> [While sleeping] I was unable to move. I also felt pressure at the base of my throat, as if something were pressing at the bottom of my neck. I was unable to open my eyes.

Diana, an administrative assistant, described her sleep paralysis like this:

> Lying in bed in the morning, thinking of getting up for work, I tried to move and could not. I was looking out of my closed eyelids and I tried to scream, but I could not.

Of course, everyone wakes up from paralysis, no matter how long it lasts, which can be anywhere from a second or two to about an hour.

When respondents in my survey became aware of how often paralysis was invading their sleeping patterns, fifty-nine percent, or 2,221 participants, said they had felt they were awake but could not move their bodies or open their eyes. About eighty-two percent, or 1,820 participants, said that paralysis made them fearful or panicky while it was occurring.

After my own near-death experience, I noticed a sudden onset of, and then a terrifying increase in, sleep paralysis in the middle of the night. No matter what I tried to do to stop it, it continued to occur.

One night, in total desperation, I decided to lie quietly, to avoid fighting it, and to ask God to show me why this was happening to me. For about thirty minutes, I lay there unable to move. While I tried not to be afraid, I begged, *Please, God, show me what's happening. I want to know, God. I will not be afraid. Please show me why I am paralyzed. Show me.*

All of a sudden, I was partially "out," sitting up in bed, my physical body under me. I could see two of me at the same time: my solid physical body, and my transparent spirit body. I instantly knew that this was an out-of-body similar to what had happened during my near-death journey. But I also knew that I was not dead; I was well and resting in bed, my body lying paralyzed below me. I turned my head and clearly saw my physical body trying to move. My eyes appeared to be wincing, trying to open.

I sat there for some time, looking at the two sets of my legs in front of me—my physical legs and my transparent legs. I could move my transparent legs, but not my physical legs. I could also see two sets of arms. My physical arms

106

were lying at my physical body's side, and my transparent spirit arms were extended in front of me.

Then I decided to ask how to make the experience stop, and a voice said, "Move your little fingers." I tried to move my little fingers, but nothing happened. Then the voice said, "Think it." Suddenly, in about a tenth of a second, I slammed back into my body with a jolt. At first I thought this solution to ending paralysis was preposterous, but consistent success proves it works!

Since then, I have taught this technique to thousands, to the great relief of those who have recalled experiencing paralysis while dreaming.

As my student, Paul, a minister, explained:

> I couldn't move. Then I managed to "move" my left little finger, and I came out of the paralysis, wide awake.

When your mind is on edge, as it might be during times of stress or excitement, you'll be more likely to recognize paralysis. When you're keenly alert as you lie down to sleep, and your body is physically exhausted from the day's activities, the circumstances are right for an out-of-body experience.

If, when you find yourself paralyzed, you choose not to think about moving your little fingers, you can fly, see a deceased relative or loved one, or go anywhere imaginable. Try to see something that you can confirm with details once you have awakened.

Rosanna, a former student who has become a friend, is a near-death experiencer who later had many significant out-of-body experiences.

Several years later, she had another near-death experience which left her comatose for five days. During that time, she knew she was out of her body. Rosanna used several of the techniques she had learned to help her retain conscious awareness of her out-of-body experience. This also helped her choose where she wanted to go, and removed her fears. Rosanna actually used the "little finger" movement to help her awaken from the coma!

Intense fear always ends the experience. Therefore, if you want to have a conscious out-of-body trip, you must control any fears that arise when sleep paralysis begins. Otherwise, you'll quickly return to your body with a jolt.

Sleep paralysis should not be confused with narcolepsy. Narcoleptics fall asleep immediately at random times—most commonly triggered by laughter. People with narcolepsy do experience a type of paralysis during these episodes, but to date, there is no indication that their sleep during paralysis involves an out-of-body experience.

Two narcoleptics told me that they were unaware of any paralysis taking place during the narcoleptic period. In fact, they were always surprised later to find they had been asleep.

Remember, when you awaken from sleep and know you can't move, you are partly out-of-body. You can control this sleep paralysis in one of two ways: either by stopping it with your "little finger" or relaxing and letting yourself enjoy an out-of-body experience. Try it—you'll love it!

KEY FOUR: AWAKENING TWICE

Sometimes people dream that they are awake, and the dream seems so real, so vivid, they're positive they really are awake. Then, they awaken a second time, and realize they've been dreaming.

When people begin recording their dreams, they learn that some of these vivid dreams are really conscious out-of-body experiences. Awakening a second time alerts them to the fact that they've just had an out-of-body experience.

Nicole, a medical assistant, joined my class in 1983. Soon afterwards, with a sigh of relief, she admitted that she had been afraid she was losing her mind until she heard out-of-body stories from her fellow students that paralleled her own. Nicole recounted one in which she awakened twice and had an unforgettable glimpse of the Light.

I was in bed asleep when I suddenly awoke for the first time. It felt as if electrical currents were passing through my body, but I thought, *Okay, let's go for it.* My arms went up as if I were going to sit up in bed. The

109

next thing I experienced was total blackness, followed by a bright Light that appeared at my left and continued to expand until my whole range of vision was filled with beautiful golden Light.

A being dressed in a luminous garment similar to a golden cowl appeared in the Light. As I focused my attention on this being, the Light slowly changed from gold to lavender.

The scene then changed to that of a ballroom. Women in gauzy pastel dresses were dancing with men in dark tuxedos. As the scene faded, I heard what seemed to be a radio with the volume turned up high. The noise sounded like a western movie, with lots of thundering hooves beating the ground. [Author's note: This is the noise often heard before one is pulled back into the body.]

The last thing I remember while being out of body was a voice in my left ear. I couldn't describe it as masculine or feminine; it had a rather strange quality. The voice merely said, "I love you." The next thing I knew, I was back in bed. Then, I awoke the second time.

Nicole says that since this experience, she no longer fears death or being out of her body. She has repeatedly succeeded in having out-of-body experiences by lying down and preparing herself to have one during the dream state.

One cause for confusion during Key Four is the fact that, when the spirit is out of body between "awakenings," people recall being able to see in great detail through closed eyelids. This leads them to believe they were actually awake, rather than out of body. In fact, some participants even told me they reached up to touch their eyelids. In every case, their eyes were tightly closed.

A respondent named Jan recalls:

> After shopping and cleaning I decided to put my head on the arm of the chair and watch TV sideways. I had no intention of closing my eyes. The next thing I knew, I could see the family room ceiling getting closer and closer. I realized it was I who was moving up!
>
> I suddenly jerked so hard that I almost fell out of the chair. Then it hit me: *How can I see the ceiling getting closer if my eyes are closed?*

A number of respondents—978, or twenty-six percent —stated that they had seen their rooms brightly lit through their closed eyelids, even though the lamps were not on and it was dark outside. During out-of-body travel, sight is made available through the mind. The physical eyes need not to be open in order to see.

KEY FIVE: LUCID DREAMING

The fifth key to having a guided out-of-body experience is becoming aware when you are having a "lucid dream."

A lucid dream occurs when you absolutely know while you're dreaming that you are "lucid," or clearly recognize that you *are* dreaming, no matter how "real" that dream might be. Once you're aware that you're dreaming, you can turn that dream into a directed out-of-body experience.

Prior to falling asleep, tell yourself that if you see yourself in a lucid dream that night, you will actually be out of body. This can be verified the next day by choosing a location or person to visit, then reporting on it later to confirm the details.

You can also prepare to have a lucid dream by telling yourself while awake that you will remember the next time you're having a particular type of dream. For example, you might say, "I'll know, when I fly in my dreams tonight, that I'm really out of body."

Say it with confidence. Then, when you know you are flying in your dream, you can guide yourself to the place you would like to see. A few people have reported that just thinking of flying during a dream caused a spontaneous out-of-body experience. Then, while they were out of body, they selected their destinations, and were delighted with their experiences.

Don, a computer analyst, wanted to have a lucid dreaming out-of-body experience ever since he'd taken my course. He knew that before falling asleep he had to suggest to himself that he would have a lucid dream, recognize it as such, and see where it took him. After a few weeks of preparing himself for the experience, he eventually had an out-of-body experience that amazed him.

I awoke to find myself out of my body, standing by my bed. I was able to see through the walls for a great distance. Then, I thought of my front yard, and I was there. Believe me, I was overwhelmed!

I'd been a little homesick for southern California, and my thoughts went to my mother, who lives there. With that, I was instantly flying fast, covering distances in just minutes that would otherwise take days.

My out-of-body experience was terminated when I met power lines in the desert. While I was fighting the power lines, I could hear myself breathing and my heart beating. Then I woke up.

I sat up for over an hour, feeling great joy that I did not understand. All I knew was that I felt on top of the world! Now I'm looking forward to the next time . . . .

Incidentally, Don's encounter with power lines is not unusual. I've found that many of my students automatically shy away from them; perhaps it's a remnant of an earthbound fear. But when brave students have actually "touched" a power line, nothing has happened to their spirit forms, and they've been able to continue on their journeys.

One startling example of a verified lucid dream truly impressed me, even after years of hearing examples from my students.

Eleven-year-old Tami, who had been having lucid dreams for some time, decided one day to visit me during one of them. I have some miniature buildings on my front porch, and one of them is a church. Inside it, I had placed a Bible, with a red string inside Psalm Twenty-two.

Shortly after visiting me while out of her body, Tami called me. "Dianne, I went inside your miniature church," she reported.

I was stunned. "You're kidding!"

"No, I'm not," she laughed. "Go outside and see. I turned the page of your Bible to Psalm Twenty-three."

No one else but I knew there was a Bible inside the miniature church. I ran outside to check Tami's story. Sure enough, the ribbon had been moved to the twenty-third Psalm. The ability to move physical matter while out of body is rare—but obviously very possible!

Below are some descriptions by people who had become aware that they were having a lucid dream.

Ofelia recalled:

> I dreamed that I left my physical body. I felt as if an extreme force was pulling me into outer space into a glowing space, where I melted into nothingness. I felt as if I knew everything that can be known.

Carol, a teacher, told me:

> I knew that I was dreaming. I was in the kitchen and noticed my daughter was still home, although I remembered I had taken her to school. I saw the

refrigerator, and the kitchen looked slightly backwards—a shower stall was in the refrigerator's place!

Suddenly, I knew I was flying out of my body. Instantly, as soon as I thought it, I was in the shower stall. I tried touching the sides of the stall with my hands, but they went through the tiles and the wall.

I enjoyed the experience thoroughly, and I didn't want it to end. I tried not to get too excited.

Then, I heard a voice from the shower saying, "*Sine qua non.*" Not knowing Latin, I later looked up its meaning: "*an essential condition, requisite or prerequisite.*" I want to do it again.

Carol knew she should control her excitement because any strong emotion can bring you back from an out-of-body experience.

If you want to experience a more conscious state during lucid dreams, know in advance, before you get out of your body, what you would like to see. Decide on it while you are awake, so that once you gain consciousness during the lucid dream, you will have some control over your destination.

KEY SIX: HANDS/FEET/CAMERA

It's easier to become aware that you're having an out-of-body experience while asleep if you give yourself a couple of clues to notice while you're out of your body. Using "hands, feet, and camera" is Key Six to help awaken your consciousness during a dream. The dream then becomes a "lucid dream," one you can guide. At that point you can select what you wish to see during the dream.

First, place a camera (working or not) on your path between your bedroom and the place where you normally enter your home. In other words, be sure you have to walk past your camera in order to get to your bed. Use the path that you would normally take leading directly into your bedroom. During the day, tell yourself, "If I see my camera during a dream, I will want to pick it up and take a picture of my dream."

Second, tell yourself aloud before sleep, while looking at your hand (or foot), "If I see my hand (or foot) during my dream, I will know that I am dreaming, and I will awaken within my dream."

These two cues will help you remember more dream material, and they might also cause a spontaneous out-of-body experience during sleep.

I myself had an unforgettable hands/feet/camera experience. Before falling asleep, I had told myself that I would recognize my lucid dream as a doorway to an out-of-body experience if I saw my hand or foot while dreaming.

Once asleep, I found myself dreaming that I was looking at a college bulletin board. When I raised my hand to follow an underlined message, I suddenly realized, *I'm out!* Then I turned and saw my Uncle Vince. I thought, *That can't be Uncle Vince,* so I turned around again, and nobody was there.

I walked over to a ramp to investigate, and that's when I saw Him. I knew without a doubt that the figure was Jesus. I joined Him, and we walked up the ramp together. Jesus asked me to look on His other side, and Uncle Vince was standing there—both beings glowing brilliantly and wearing long white robes. Suddenly, a cup of water appeared in Jesus's right hand. He passed the water to Uncle Vince, and I knew at that moment that my uncle would die and join Jesus very soon.

A few days later, my mother told me that my Uncle Vince had suddenly passed away.

Patti remembers with excitement her hand/foot/camera experience.

I was floating over the beach past some people. I came to some stairs and began to climb up to a platform, but my feet went through the stairs! I looked at my hands, which were completely vivid. Instantly, I felt in control of my experience.

Often, when people are out of body, they create a vehicle of some type—an airplane, car, train, hot-air balloon, or boat—to get to their destination. Wendy recalls:

I was having a lucid dream of being on an old sailing ship. All of a sudden, I was in my own little boat and paddling with my arms. I saw my hands and remembered: *I am out of my body!* I was so excited that my little boat began to fly! I could see the stars and the moon, and its reflection in the mist. I was flying along the coast.

Laura describes her experience as follows:

While dreaming, I saw my camera. At first I thought, *Why is this here?* Then I remembered and tried to pick it up, and my hand went through it! I was still shocked to be conscious and out of my body. So I sat down at the top of my stairs to try to absorb what was happening. I decided I wanted more proof.

I wanted to see part of my physical body, so I looked through the doorway and could see my [physical] hand just off the bed. Going down the stairs, I decided to play and I tumbled down the last half on purpose. I felt light and "cushy." I went up the stairs again, then back toward my body. I jumped backwards into my body on purpose.

Recently I called John, a former student, because I wanted to ask his permission to use a piece of artwork he'd done for me years ago depicting an out-of-body experience. He was surprised to hear from me, since it had been about ten years since we'd seen each other.

The night John had presented the art to me in class, he'd mentioned that he'd had a very vivid dream about me. I asked him if he wanted to share it with the class, and he said he'd seen that I had purchased a car and that my new key chain had a "G" on it. John's dream was very accurate; in fact, my keys were hidden in my hand. Then I revealed to the class that indeed there was a "GM" on my new key ring for the car I had purchased earlier that week.

Once I arrived home, I had a chance to really look at his artwork, and thought it unusual for a young man to have such talent. I sent him a "thank you" note.

John told me that he still had my thank-you note and asked if I remembered what I'd written. I recalled that I had thought I should write something about his future because he would surely go places. John reminded me that I had written: "I'm sure you'll work at Disney one day." He told me this message had given him the confidence to continue his art—and that he was now working for Walt Disney Studios!

KEY SEVEN: ANGELS, RADIANT BEINGS, AND THE LIGHT

The final key to recognizing an out-of-body experience is the viewing of a radiant being, or departed loved one, or actually glimpsing "the Light."

While this Key can lead to one of the most thrilling experiences, it is not as easy to attain. You'll have a greater chance of seeing these celestial visions if you tend to sleep for long, uninterrupted periods. The longer you sleep, the more REM dream time you'll have, which is when the all-important paralysis stage occurs. At this time, angels, deceased relatives, or spirits were seen by one hundred ninety-nine of my respondents.

The spirit, radiant angelic being, or deceased relative usually appears near the foot of the bed, most often in transparent form, but occasionally solid, frequently glowing, and always as a bearer of tidings, usually positive. All who reported seeing deceased relatives said loved ones communicated telepathically, indicating that they were happy and that all would be well.

The most authentic cases of contact are those in which the deceased relative provides information about something previously unknown to the dreamer which later proves to be true.

Many of my students have not only seen deceased relatives, they have even resolved problems with them. They also report feeling extremely relieved when they discover how positive the deceased relative behaves. Dr. Stephen La Berge, a pioneer in lucid dream research at Stanford University, has found in lucid dreaming "a significant potential for emotional healing, such as resolving a conflict with a loved one who had died."

The absolute wonder of seeing an angel was experienced by Linda, an insurance clerk, while she was out of her body.

> When I was seven years old, we had a visit from some relatives. My mother went to the car to see them off. I was very tired, and I remember wishing that they would hurry. I must have left my body, when something told me to look up and to my left. There was an angel floating quietly in the night sky. It appeared to be a female angel with short, curly golden hair. She wore a

robe in the most beautiful shade of green, and even had large white wings. Her entire body was illuminated. She was holding a book in her hands and reading from it; her lips were moving.

John, a calligrapher and artist, was keeping a journal of his dreams and was eager to see the Light. This became his goal whenever he meditated or slept. One day, while meditating in front of a mirror, he began thinking about the loving Light of God and finally gathered enough confidence to look in the mirror.

While I was still sitting down, I looked down at my arms and legs. They looked strange, like blue gelatin. I was out of my body! Then, I stood up and saw my reflection in the mirror. It looked dark bluish and I was in silhouette, even though I was looking at the mirror full face!

[Author's note: Often, while out of body, people see themselves in clothing different from what they are wearing. Sometimes they will be in a white gown, typical of that seen in near-death experiences, or they may be wearing another color. Furthermore, mirrors viewed by those out of body do not always reflect Earth reality.]

As I looked down, I saw my whole body surrounded by white Light. I felt myself rising up past the mirror until I felt a soft, gentle thump on my head. It was as if the ceiling were made of foam rubber. There was no gravity, just weightlessness. It was unlike anything I've ever felt before.

Then I felt as if someone had grabbed me around my waist. I was quickly turned around horizontally so I could feel the ceiling against my back. I was again turned around and pushed back into bed. I woke up not scared, but a bit amused about the whole event. In retrospect, I think a spirit guide was helping me return to my body.

Deanne, a private investigator, reports:

I was out of my body, flying in a jet to see my deceased Aunt Betsy. In the plane I saw Marilyn, a woman in Dr. Morrissey's class. I noticed that her husband was not with her. I saw Aunt Betsy and I was aware of how good she looked. Then I awakened.

Later, in class, I told Marilyn of my out-of-body experience. She said that on the same night on which I had had my out-of-body experience, she had dreamed she was on a jet plane without her husband.

What Deanne and Marilyn experienced, of course, was a simultaneous out-of-body experience.

If you wish to meet a loved one in a lucid dream, all you need to do is have an intense desire to see the person as you drift off to sleep. Think only of your loved one as you enter sleep. Know that when you fall asleep you will be with that person. Remember, there is no past, present, or future during an out-of-body experience, so it doesn't matter where your friend or loved one is in time or space. Be vigorous and persistent in your efforts and you will succeed.

Other survey respondents report having seen radiant beings or deceased relatives. Al described his experience this way:

> While I was in the hospital for an appendix operation, the man sharing the room with me had had an operation for cancer of the stomach. A couple of days before being released, I was just relaxing, lying on the bed. All of a sudden I found myself sitting in the chair at the foot of the bed, looking back at myself. Then I saw two individuals glide through the closed door. One was wearing the robe of a monk, and at his side was another man dressed all in white, with golden hair. Both men were holding a candle, and their hands were in a praying position. They were surrounded by a golden Light.
>
> The man in the bed next to mine was making groaning noises because he needed help, so I rang for the nurse. Later, I found out that he had passed away.

Simply seeing a radiant being or loved one might jolt you awake, as your subconscious mind recognizes this as an unusual occurrence. In other words, since we are unaccustomed to seeing angels or radiant beings while awake, we register the oddity of the event even while we are out of body during sleep. As soon as you notice something peculiar in your dream, your mind will become aware that it's in a dream state, and you'll awaken within the dream.

Tell yourself before you retire that, while dreaming, you will be sharply aware of things that seem out of place. Then, unusual occurrences will awaken you within your dream.

Maria, a grocery clerk, saw the Light during an out-of-body journey:

> I was sound asleep. Suddenly, I was awake and sitting straight up in bed. I noticed the whole house was drenched in a blue Light. I felt someone in my room, but I didn't see anybody. I got out of bed and walked toward the door. When I got to the doorway, I turned around and saw myself asleep in my bed.
>
> I felt strange, as if I were in two places at once. The blue Light was brighter in the hall, and I felt myself call out to my stepmother; I could see her asleep in her bed. Now, the blue Light was everywhere. I called again to my stepmother, but she didn't hear me. It seemed to take forever to get to her door, but I could neither get in nor out of her room. Then I woke up.

In this case, Maria's vivid out-of-body experience turned back into a dream. Maria was evidently out of body at first, saw her home, saw her stepmother in bed, and saw the Light. Then the out-of-body experience turned into a dream over which Maria had less control.

Because she was in the paralysis stage, she called to her stepmother but could not be heard. Nor could she move to her stepmother's door easily. As soon as she began feeling frustrated, she awakened.

Thomas, a dentist, remembered seeing Light in an out-of-body journey.

> Apparently, I fell asleep but was awakened by a presence in the room. I felt frightened and remember having my eyes shut, but was able to see the darkened room quite clearly. I saw the dark outline of a human body, a shadow. I could also see a brilliant Light coming from behind my head. I was not afraid.
>
> Then, I saw a tunnel of Lights. I was awakened by two people, one of them a woman. I felt lightness and tingling.

Paul, a minister, wanted to see the Light and finally saw a radiant being, or guide, while he was asleep.

> I rose up out of my body and traveled through space, where I met a guide waiting for me in a large, white marble room. People were sitting, all of them wearing white, waiting for their teacher. The guide looked at me and said, "This is where you are coming next!" He spoke without words. Suddenly, I was back in my body.

Ellen, a teacher, was awakened from sleep by a floral scent. Looking out her bedroom door, she could see a Light coming from her baby's bedroom.

> I walked toward the room and the Light. I had no fear. It was warm, and the floral scent was becoming stronger. On entering the tiny bedroom, I saw my husband's grandmother gazing at the baby. The Light was Grandmother!
>
> She looked at me and then at my baby, and said, "She's beautiful. I will always be here for her." She patted the baby gently on the bottom as she stood next to her crib and she told me to go back to bed. I did, but sitting down on the bed, I thought, *But I want to be with her.*
>
> I went back immediately, but she was gone. The room was warm and still held the floral scent. The baby was awake and making soft cooing sounds. I felt warm inside.

John, an attorney, hadn't really remembered a dream since he was a child. He diligently wrote down his dreams in a journal, and the next week eagerly shared his first vivid dream with our class. He then asked, grinning, "How do any of you get any sleep with so much to watch?"

He describes his experience as follows:

> I went to a friend's house in Santa Barbara and lay down to relax. Suddenly, I was aware that the room had changed. The entire room was glowing, and there, in my vision, was an angel. She was glowing and

wearing shades of red. Everything was glowing red, and I saw her clearly. She was shorter than I, and filled with goodness. It was as if she were representing all the goodness in the world. When I awakened from my out-of-body experience, I was emotionally blown away that this could have happened to me!

Why did the radiant being wear red, rather than white or gold? No one can predict or explain the colors they will see when out of body, but John's sense of the radiant being's incredible "goodness" strongly indicates an angelic presence.

Many of us have felt the presence of our angels ever since we were children; as adults, however, we tend to explain away the feeling that an angel may be near. The truth is, our angels are always with us. Although we need not even believe in them in order to see one, the more we acknowledge our angels, the more we'll see wonderful things happening around us as our angels enhance our lives.

Here's how you can reach out to your angel:

• Before falling asleep, lie on your back and don't move. Stay very quiet, without even blinking. Simply breathe. You may think about anything you wish, but do not move your body.

• In time, with your eyes still closed, you'll feel as if you're paralyzed, even though you may tell yourself that you can move. (This type of paralysis is not the same as the sleep paralysis you enter during REM sleep, although it does feel similar.) The ability to reach this level of consciousness will depend on your personal rate of relaxation, and your ability to resist distractions.

• While lying quietly, mentally ask to see or feel the presence of your angel. Above all, continue lying very still with your eyes closed, not moving at all. Tell yourself that you're going to remain awake and resist sleep. After lying there for a while, you might see a sudden burst of bright, swirling colors, geometric forms, or lattices and colors mixed together. Or, you might see only the normal blackness that results from closing your eyes until your angel arrives.

• When your angel appears, you might feel a touch on your hand, shoulder, or head, or you might feel your foot being tugged. If you're afraid at any time, everything will stop instantly.

Angels are telepathic and can instantly pass information into your mind. They sound just as humans do when they speak, but their voices may sound loud within your head. Their voices might seem to be coming from right beside you, or right next to your ear. The voice you hear will not be your own voice or your inner voice, but a distinct voice you have probably never heard before. Yet, it may seem familiar to you, probably because you tuned into your angel when you were a child. Unfortunately, somewhere between childhood and adulthood, many people stop believing in angels.

Fortunately, even though we usually don't see them, angels interact with adults all the time.

A honeymoon couple in their car began to pass a large truck in front of them. As they pulled out, they realized that another car was passing at the same time, and knew they were not going to get around the truck without colliding with the approaching car. The couple was very frightened, and for about one second each of them felt a small lapse in time. Suddenly, their vehicle was *lifted back into their own lane* in front of the truck they'd been attempting to pass! This phenomenon was, of course, absolutely impossible to explain by any rational means. It certainly appears to have been an example of divine intervention.

I truly believe that when people still have work to do that will help others, angels work special miracles to spare those individuals from life-threatening events.

If you feel the need, ask for help from your angel. Then, believe that your angel will take care of the situation, and tell yourself that since you've asked for help, a miracle will occur at the right time. You will soon come to realize that there are no accidents or coincidences. Life's challenges will make you stronger, not weaker. When you are faced with hardships in life, remind yourself that you've become a stronger person, a better spirit, and a more intuitive soul with a more inspired heart.

Your angel loves you more than you can possibly imagine, and is ready to help you. When you let this love in, you will be transformed. You can do it; the Light of the angels is everywhere.

Review

The following Seven Keys will help you recognize when you are having an out-of-body experience during sleep. You can then guide your experience toward the Light, or in whatever direction you choose.

1. Watch for the **jolt** as you begin to fall asleep. Note especially when you think you moved, but later find that you did not. On these occasions, you have been out-of-body.

2. Be aware, before you go to bed, that you might feel as if you're vibrating from head to foot. If **vibrations** begin, relax and just allow them to occur, knowing that you are moving into an out-of-body experience.

3. Watch for the **paralysis** stage that occurs spontaneously during sleep. At this point, you will already be partly out of your body. If, at that time, you think strongly about someone you love, you'll fly to wherever that person is and see him or her. You will also know that you are asleep and conscious within your dream.

You can also lie on your bed with your eyes closed and imitate the paralysis stage. By staying awake and keeping your body completely still, you can bring on a similar state of paralysis. From that point on, you can will yourself to have a conscious out-of-body journey.

It is during paralysis that healing techniques for yourself or others work best. Remember not to become too emotional when you are out of your body, as this alone can cause the experience to end before you are ready.

4. Begin to notice occasions on which you find yourself **awakening twice.** In other words, the first time you think you are awake, you will be awake within your dream. Right after that, you will physically awaken. You might need a moment to realize that you were not out of bed after all, but still asleep, even though the experience seemed so real!

5. You can use **lucid dreaming** to direct your dreams and bring yourself to a chosen person, situation, or destination. Guiding your dreams is not only possible, but a time-tested, scientific reality. This important technique can help you create a memorable out-of-body experience— and possibly bring you into the presence of loved ones on the Other Side, angelic beings, and even the Light itself.

6. You can recognize a lucid dream by cueing yourself to see your **hand or foot or camera** during a dream. When this occurs, you'll be aware that you're dreaming, and you can then guide your dream.

Place a camera where you'll see it when you enter your bedroom, and tell yourself before you go to bed that, while dreaming, you will pick up the camera when you pass it, and "take a picture of your dream."

Using the device of the camera has two purposes. First, you might find that when you pick up the camera, your hand goes right through it. The oddity of seeing your hand go through a solid object can trigger your awareness that you're out of your body.

Second, the camera can help you remember your dream when you awaken in the morning because you "took a picture" of it while you were asleep.

7. You can expect that once you are having an out-of-body experience during sleep, you'll be able to **meet a radiant angelic being or see the Light.**

This experience will truly change your life. When it occurs, you will know without doubt that you and the Light are eternally connected. Your angel will pour Light into you and envelop you in love.

A final tip, most important for quick success, is to record your dreams daily in a journal. Not only will you recognize when you may have had an out-of-body experience, but you'll be training your subconscious to notice what types of dreams you're having every night. Journaling is an extremely powerful way to program your subconscious mind to recognize when you're out of body.

These Seven Keys can take you where you've never gone before—and bring you safely back, again and again!

Part IV

Returning From The Light

6

You'll Never Be the Same

JUST AFTER LOUIS, MY NEIGHBOR, PASSED AWAY, I was fortunate enough to see him one last time. I was just pulling into my driveway when I saw him standing in front of his home. He was smiling, wearing a white shirt and blue pants; for just an instant, he looked as if he were still alive. Then it hit me: *How can I see him? He's dead!*

I could hardly believe my eyes. Quickly, I drove into the garage, jumped out of the car, and dashed outside looking toward Louis's home. He was gone, but I waved vigorously anyway; he might still be there, I thought, even if he was no longer visible. I'm sure that when I die again, I'll see him, and then I can ask him whether he saw me wave.

How was I able to see my departed neighbor? I suspect it's because I've had so many out-of-body journeys. People who have had significant near-death or guided out-of-body experiences often tend to develop new intuitive abilities, including precognition, telepathy, and clairvoyance.

In fact, once they learn to guide their dreams, many people use these abilities to locate missing persons or pets, or meet with a deceased loved one.

Several years ago, a woman whose daughter was missing asked me to help locate her. I agreed to try and attempted for several nights to find the young woman while I was out of body, focusing on a photograph I had been given. Eventually, I succeeded in locating her, and reported that I had seen the daughter in a small shack in a park northeast of her home. A man named David was with her. The mother called me several days later and gratefully informed me that I had been completely accurate.

I'm sure that the loved ones of missing persons could find them more easily than I could, since they know the lost individuals so well, and can keep a clear image of them in their minds. It's more difficult for me to search for someone I've never met, as it's quite a challenge to stay focused on an unfamiliar face.

If you wish to locate a specific person or object, use your out-of-body journeys to help you reach your objective. Before you go to bed, tell yourself that when you awaken the next morning, you'll know where to find what you are seeking. Then, begin writing down your dreams the next morning. With persistence, your chances of success will increase.

Remember, when you leave your body during sleep, you can glimpse the past, the present, or the future. Once you're aware that you're dreaming, you can observe past events being replayed in your dreams. In fact, I can personally attest that miracles really do happen in the dream state.

The first time I used an out-of-body experience to find a missing pet was after I returned from a vacation, and learned that Tuffy had climbed the fence during a thunderstorm. He hadn't returned, and I was distraught. Every day I looked for him in my local animal shelters.

Finally, in exasperation and despair, I decided to try to see Tuffy one night while I was out of my body. I found myself in a dream, running after him and calling his name. He was limping, which worried me, as I knew Tuffy was in good health and had never limped before. Suddenly, I knew that I was dreaming and that Tuffy was running on a street in front of me, still alive.

About four days later, I had an out-of-body experience in which a woman who loved animals appeared to me. She told me not to give up, saying that I would indeed find my dog and that it would be "a very loving day." I wondered what she meant by that.

In the dream, I had the sense that when I found him, Tuffy would be able to see me in living color! That surprised me because, like most people, I believed that dogs could see only in black and white.

139

Exactly six weeks later, on Valentine's Day, I was walking through a dog shelter when I heard a familiar bark. I ran to the sound, and there he was! Tuffy had lost two-thirds of his body weight, and the pads of his feet were bloody. But he was otherwise fine and very happy to see me. And I certainly had found him on "a very loving day." I had continued searching for him as long as my out-of-body experiences showed me that Tuffy was still alive.

Later, while checking the accuracy of my dream information, I was pleased to learn that American Kennel Club researchers have discovered that dogs actually do see colors, as well as black and white. The hues look different than they do to humans. For example, dogs can't tell the difference between yellow-green and yellow, or between orange and red, but they can tell the difference between those colors and white. Dogs do, in fact, see indigo, blue, and violet and can differentiate among them.

Should your pet ever go astray, here's a tip that might speed its return. Remember that an animal's ability to pick up scents far exceeds a human's ability. Therefore, you might want to place an unwashed nightgown or set of worn pajamas outside your house. This will help your lost pet pick up your scent. Your nightclothes will work best because they've come in direct contact with your skin. A pet that's close by can sniff its way home.

Precognition, the ability to see events in the future, is a natural part of many people's lives, but most of us pass it off as coincidence until we discover that the foreseen events are actually coming true. This gift seems to be enhanced by out-of-body travel.

Precognition often appears in dreams. A woman named Orea had an out-of-body experience in which she saw a dining table beautifully set, but without food. English soldiers jumped across it, then sat down and guarded it. She continues on to describe her dream:

> The table was decorated elegantly with beautiful dishes, shining silver, and crystal, but no guests were allowed. There was no smell of food. I was up at the ceiling looking down and thinking, *I'll have to remember this one.*

> Two days later, I volunteered to be a wheelchair pusher for a trip to Olivera Street. The tour included a visit to the Avila House. As we went up the ramp, I saw the dining room. It had a guard rail across it, and a woman stood there, watching the table.

> I told her that I'd dreamed of this room, but wondered where the cups and saucers were. She said, without any prodding from me, "No one is allowed in this area. Food is not allowed, either. The dishes are here in the cupboard." They were the exact place settings I'd seen while out of my body during my dream.

Sometimes prophetic dreams can leave people with regrets. One woman told me of her dismay after having a vivid lucid dream in which her girlfriend was dying in a car crash on the highway in a particular location. The next day, when she saw her friend, she thought about sharing her dream, but did not. The day after they met, her friend died in an accident in the very spot the woman had seen in her dream.

Could she have saved her? It's impossible to say, but the woman was devastated that she hadn't begged her friend to drive more carefully that day.

Since my out-of-body experiences began, I have become sensitive to forthcoming earthquakes. A woman has appeared several times in my dreams to let me know about earthquakes before they happen.

Before a 1992 quake in San Bernardino, California, this woman came to me in a dream and prepared me for a huge earthquake. Two weeks before it occurred, I tied down all my breakables and attached my bookcases to the walls. When my husband noticed that I had moved his stereo from its original location, he asked me what was going on. I told him about the impending quake and that it would register at least 7.0 on the Richter scale, and that I assumed he wouldn't want his stereo to fall on his head while he was sleeping.

Later, when my housekeeper asked what I was doing, I told her that an earthquake would take place somewhere in San Bernardino in about two weeks. The Landers quake in San Bernardino occurred one and one-half weeks later and measured 7.5 on the Richter scale.

Sometimes I physically feel an earthquake coming. About two days before a large event, I become extremely nauseated. This lasts from a few seconds to several minutes.

One Sunday morning while I was playing cards with my friends Gerd, Annabelle, and Patti, I became suddenly nauseated, and Patti said, "Oh, no! What's going to happen?" I told her that I sensed an earthquake reaching at least 5.0 or 6.0 on the Richter scale, which would occur north of us by late Tuesday. The quake occurred the next day, January 17, 1994, in the Northridge section of Los Angeles, and reached 6.8 on the Richter scale.

Before I was married, my husband was extremely skeptical about my ability to predict earthquakes, but after I made several accurate predictions, he became a believer. Now, months can go by between predictions, but the feeling of nausea I get continues to be uncannily accurate.

I believe that people who sense earthquakes before they happen are somehow picking up the electromagnetic shifts in the Earth that precede these upheavals. In controlled studies, scientists have found that the behavior of animals changes radically when they are subjected to changes in the magnetic field. It's possible that humans are affected, too, but rarely connect their symptoms with impending quakes.

I feel it's highly likely that survivors of near-death experiences are more sensitive to electromagnetic fields when they return to their bodies—which may explain why their watches sometimes fail when they wear them. In fact, since my near-death experience, all my watches—battery or wind-up—stop working when I put them on. Researchers have since discovered this is a common side-effect of the near-death experience.

The night before the 1989 San Francisco earthquake, I told my sister I sensed a large quake would occur the next day in California. I happened to be on the phone the next day with a San Francisco travel agent when she told me an earthquake had just occurred.

Before China's earthquake in 1989, I dreamed I was in a store, standing at the cash register waiting to pay for an item. The woman behind the counter spoke to me in an Asian language, and I couldn't understand what she was saying. Suddenly, an Asian man appeared next to me and handed me a Chinese-American dictionary. When I opened it, I saw written in large print: "earthquake seven point zero at four-thirty." I awoke suddenly, and shared the dream with my husband.

The next night, I lectured before about forty-five people. A woman asked me if I ever received impressions of negative events; she said she got headaches right before earthquakes. I told her about my dreams concerning earthquakes and mentioned the China dream of the previous night. The earthquake in China occurred a few days later and was only slightly off from the information I had received in my dream; it occurred close to 4:30 and was 7.3 in intensity.

People who have a precognitive awareness of such events need to know that these sensitivities will probably remain with them. Hundreds of men and women have reported strange feelings or severe headaches the day before an earthquake and have experienced these symptoms more than once. They always tell me that headaches are otherwise extremely rare for them.

Several times since my near-death experience, I've had out-of-body experiences during which I've seen events before they happened. Usually, my glimpses of the future are of positive events, but even when they're negative, they always prove informative.

The night before an oil tanker went aground in January, 1993, spilling a huge amount of oil into the North Sea, I had an out-of-body experience during a lucid and extremely vivid dream. I was walking through a parking lot when I suddenly knew I was dreaming. I was shocked to see dying birds and trees all around me. Thousands of small hummingbirds were falling to the ground and only some of the larger birds were still able to fly.

Suddenly, Jesus appeared in the sky above me. I felt overwhelmed and humbled by His presence, and He said sadly, "Look what they have done to my birds and my trees."

As I saw how the world was being destroyed by thoughtless individuals, I felt great sadness. I knew that He was telling me telepathically that the building I was walking toward was closely involved with this event. Suddenly, I awakened with a loud buzzing in my head. After I shared my out-of-body experience with my husband, I fell asleep again.

As soon as morning came, I drove to the parking lot I had seen in my dream, approached the building, and read the sign in front of it. The building was an oil refining and processing plant.

Later that morning, when my husband telephoned to tell me that he'd heard a radio announcement confirming my dream, I was distressed, but not surprised. An oil tanker had run aground off the Shetland Islands, killing more birds than any other oil spill in the world's history.

Lynn, a student of mine, reported feeling a similar grief for the world's misfortunes during an out-of-body experience. She describes it this way:

> I was sitting on a sofa in the home of a friend when I heard a ringing in my ears. My vision began to blur and a mist appeared in front of me. Pictures of my whole life began to flash before my eyes. Everything was in black and white, the good and the bad. Then a peace came. I felt a Presence with me, comforting me, enveloping me in pure love, in brilliant white Light.
>
> Cleansed by it, I passed through it. Beyond the Light was a field of grass dotted with wildflowers. The sky was incredibly blue, with white cottony clouds. Seagulls glided carelessly and butterflies fluttered everywhere. But I also had visions of great battles, famines, and unspeakable agonies in the world. I felt responsible. The next thing I knew, I was back in my friend's living room sitting on the sofa.
>
> On the way back home that day, I saw the world through new eyes: graffiti and trash everywhere, road

workers tearing into the earth to make new roads, and the sad and tired faces of people. I began to cry and felt responsible for the state of the world.

Lynn's vision was grim. But many visions received during lucid dreams can bring life-enhancing—and even historic—results!

• Albert Einstein's lucid dreams helped him develop the theory of relativity.

• Friedrich August Kekul, a chemist, discovered the molecular arrangement of benzene in a dream, a discovery that has been called "the most brilliant prediction to be found in the whole range of organic chemistry."

• Wolfgang Amadeus Mozart wrote symphonies that he recalled from his dreams.

• Richard Wagner wrote *Der Ring des Nibelungen* after seeing it in a dream.

• Robert Louis Stevenson wrote stories of "little people" he had seen in his dreams.

• Dmitri Ivanovich Mendeleev, the brilliant Russian chemist, received information for his Periodic Table of Elements in a dream, including knowledge about elements that had not yet been discovered.

• Salvador Dali's painting, "Persistence of Memory," was created as the result of a dream.

• Igor Stravinsky often "slept on a problem." He awakened from one dream with *The Rites of Spring* fully formed in his mind.

John Steinbeck said, "It is a common experience that a problem difficult at night is resolved in the morning after the committee of sleep has worked on it."

Remote viewing is another unusual ability that can develop after having out-of-body experiences. This is the gift of being able to see something, or to receive strong, accurate feelings about its appearance, without seeing it with one's physical eyes. This is relatively simple to learn, and those who attempt it usually find that, with practice, they can do it quite easily. No prior belief or special ability, psychic or otherwise, is necessary for success.

You can try remote viewing by placing, face down on a table, an open magazine that has a wide variety of pictures in it. You must not look at the contents of the magazine before this attempt. Pretend that your eyes are in the best place to see the pictures—probably under the table, looking up through the table to the pictures facing downward.

Colored pictures seem to be the easiest to see; black and white pictures are a little more difficult, and cartoons are the most difficult to see accurately. Now, try to "see" the picture in your mind. It may take several tries, but you'll be pleasantly surprised when you find that practice *does* make perfect!

7

Ready to Live Again, Unafraid to Die

ONE DAY I RECEIVED A CALL FROM ANDREW, whose distress had brought him to the brink of suicide. His only brother had drowned, and his body had never been recovered. This so disturbed Andrew that he desperately wanted to learn if his brother was all right on the Other Side. He believed that he had to take his own life in order to be able to contact his brother again.

I suggested using an out-of-body experience during sleep to reconnect with his lost brother, and urged him to watch for the Seven Keys to seeing the Light. I emphasized that Andrew think only about his brother as he drifted off to sleep and let no other thoughts enter his mind. He was to feel confident that God would give him a message from his brother.

A few days later, Andrew telephoned me again. Deeply shaken, he told me he would never have believed what had happened since we had spoken. During a lucid dream, a very loving man suddenly appeared before him who seemed to know his dead brother. Andrew sensed that his brother was standing behind this man.

The man asked Andrew if he wanted to talk to his brother, and at this moment, he knew that his brother was truly in Heaven and happy. Simultaneously, he received a glimpse of what Heaven was like. Andrew said he could no longer even think of taking his life, as he now realized how important it was for him to help others.

Those who have out-of-body experiences rarely come back with a death wish. On the contrary, they live life to the fullest, and enjoy their journeys so much, they eagerly await the next one. These travelers also come away from their experiences no longer fearing death.

Parents whose children have died are in particular need of reassurance about death. Once, I spoke before a convention of Compassionate Friends, a support group for parents whose children had died, and shared my near-death experience with hundreds of parents. I was particularly touched by one woman's letter that arrived a few days later. She revealed how relieved and at peace she now felt, knowing that there is no pain when we die. All near-death survivors I have met attest to this release of pain once on the Other Side.

My own near-death experience not only helped me overcome my fear of death, but gave me a special eagerness and enthusiasm for life I never possessed before I "died" in 1977.

Before my near-death experience, there were many things in my life that I had wanted to do, but was afraid to try. They were just too frightening, like learning to ski or going glider flying. Previously, I had worried about getting hurt or even dying if I participated in such activities. But after my near-death experience, I found it easy to learn things that had previously frightened me.

My friend, Judy, had long begged me to go ice skating with her, but I had always said, "No, I'll probably die trying." Judy kept reassuring me that I'd be fine, and after my near-death experience I finally took her up on her offer. While getting onto the ice, I joked that the worst thing that could happen to me was that I might die twice!

Of course, I'm not eager to try the impossible, or attempt something that could easily cause my death. I don't want to die—I know I have a lot to live for!

On rare occasions, people have called me and said they wanted to die because they heard how wonderful life is on the Other Side. Their lives feel so hopeless, they say, that killing themselves will relieve their pain. This attitude always saddens me, as do questions such as, "By sharing how wonderful death is, might that not make someone want to die?"

Of course, near-death experiencers may look forward to dying again someday, but they also understand that all of us have a specific purpose here on Earth, and we must complete it before we die. I explain that God has given us the gift of Life, and we should respect it and treasure the opportunities awaiting us on This Side. I always encourage those contemplating suicide to get medical and/or spiritual help. Furthermore, I suggest that when they are dreaming, they can learn to see the Light. Once they do, they will be convinced of the importance of their lives.

Interestingly, those who attempt suicide and have a near-death experience do not attempt to take their lives again. Once you enter the Light, you realize how important your life really is to you—as well as to God.

ASSISTANCE IN CROSSING OVER

There's a good chance that most of us will eventually witness someone else's death. You may be at the bedside of a loved one who's about to pass over, either from an accident, injury, disease, or old age. And, because of our planet's excessively crowded conditions, I believe our biological systems will create an increasing number of new viruses and bacteria. People are rather like fish: if you put too many of them in a container, they begin to die, no matter how much you feed them.

Whatever the cause of death, we can help the dying. Many near-death experiencers later enter hospice programs to reassure and prepare dying patients before they cross over to the Other Side.

My own near-death experience taught me that if I could live a billion blissful years on Earth, I could never feel as wonderful as I did when I was on the Other Side. Therefore, I always encourage loved ones of those who are dying to tell them to let go and walk into the Light.

Susan, a student of mine, told me she had wanted to walk over to her dying mother and tell her not to be afraid, but to walk into the Light. She resisted the impulse, however, concerned that others in the room would think her behavior unusual. A nurse was sitting beside her mother, watching the woman struggle for breath. She finally leaned over to her patient and whispered in her ear, "Walk into the Light," after which the dying woman took one or two additional breaths and passed over.

Afterwards, Susan, crying, went into the hallway outside the hospital room, accompanied by the nurse. Tearfully, Susan asked the nurse what had prompted her to say those words to her mother.

The nurse replied, "During an angiogram I died, and while I was dead, God told me that the reason I was a nurse was to help people cross over."

Susan then wished she had been the one to tell her mother to walk into the Light when she crossed over. But she was also grateful for the woman's words of reassurance, which echoed those she had already learned. Next time, she would feel confident enough to use them herself.

Often, the dying patient wants to hold onto life only for the sake of the survivors. I assure you, a dying person will be overjoyed once on the Other Side. Remember, none of us dies; we only change form.

You, too, can help someone who has had a death in the family. There is an old Finnish saying I heard when visiting that country—"Only a few have returned from Death's domain." Near-death and out-of-body travelers have an opportunity to see the edge of Death's domain, and are the best candidates to help the dying and their survivors.

In North America, most people vigorously try to conceal the reality of death. *Thanatophobia,* or fear of death, runs rampant as we do everything we can to camouflage death from the observer. Did you know that flowers were first used at funerals to cover unwanted odors from the corpse? Although we shrink from reminders of our own mortality, the Latin phrase, *memento mori,* means, "Remember, you must die!"

The early Egyptians believed that those who refused to look at death had a much harder time living life. Mark Twain said, "How hard it is that we have to die—a strange complaint to come from the mouths of people who have had to live."

William Penn once said, "He that lives forever, never fears dying." Yet, when we live in the Light, we are unafraid to let death take our hands when the time is right.

DOES TIME REALLY EXIST?

In death, I learned there was no time, and no word for time. Our terms, "past," "present," and "future" blended together, coexisting on one plane at the same moment as a harmonious part of the whole.

I have often been asked what timelessness feels like on the Other Side. You can best understand it by trying to remember a very special event from your life, and then consciously hold every flickering memory of its beginning, development, and conclusion every second of every day and night.

If this were possible, you would soon begin to feel as if the event belonged to the current moment and had become part of you. It would no longer feel as if it existed in the past, because every aspect of the event would have been brought into the present.

Add to these memories your exact feelings when the event first happened; then, add more memories, over and over again, just as you felt when it originally occurred. There would be no sense of time, because all memories would be in the "now."

When near-death experiencers have their Life Reviews, they witness all the events at the same time, as if they were "above" these visions looking down at them.

Another simile would be the act of observing a film. Imagine you're aware of the plot of the movie you're watching. You're then shown each frame of the movie simultaneously. This is an approximation of how the Life Review appears, and the timelessness in which it exists.

Prior to my near-death experience, time represented a prolonging of responsibilities, all strung together until completed. Time was a drudgery. But my new awareness of time gave me a fresh outlook on life, on goals, and on boredom. I learned that "accomplishment" meant living in the moment.

Now I get much more out of life because I focus on the "now." I call my new way of life "a quest for freedom," which I consider the opposite of "stuckdum," where I used to exist. No longer is life boring or filled with needless responsibilities—it's filled instead with my choices and priorities.

The Light taught me that we can select our responsibilities, as well as the times we are unproductive or still. I now prefer to call these still moments, "tacets." In music, the instruction to tacet is when the composer tells the musician to be silent for a specific period of time. This prescribes a measure of rest.

In essence, we are the composers of our lives; we direct the times we play and the times we rest. Thus, there is no boredom, no "unproductive" moment; we decide to play, or we decide to tacet. When we realize that we compose each moment, we learn to truly live in that moment.

Several years ago, I met a woman diagnosed with terminal cancer. She told me that her physician had given her only twenty-eight days to live. She was deeply dismayed, feeling she needed additional time to get the rest of her life together. I loaned her the book, *Getting Well Again,* by Dr. Carl Simonton, and told her that no one but God knows when we will actually die. She lived two more years and made the most of them, amazing her doctor with her tenacity for life.

After my near-death experience, I pondered the absence of time on the Other Side. I was fascinated by the fact that those who died and came back always claimed, "When I was dead, there was no time." I wondered how time as we know it could exist if there was no time on the Other Side.

I started reading everything I could find about time and discovered that it exists only in our minds. Humans, not God, created time. Things do move in the universe, but the measurement of the duration of that movement, or "time," was a man-made invention.

The sundial, our first "clock", isn't really a clock. Its shadow shows us how the Earth moves in comparison with the position of the stars. Later timepieces modeled after the sundial really indicated the Earth's rotation—not the passage of time itself.

I'm convinced that, to understand "time," a simple experiment in relativity will be of benefit. When I teach courses on out-of-body travel, I invite a couple to walk together across the room. Then, I'll ask everyone exactly what they saw moving. The couple, while walking, will claim to see the walls moving past them; the seated students will see the couple moving. If an astronaut on the moon were to look down on us, he or she would see the Earth moving. It's all a matter of perspective—it's all relative to where you are.

Albert Einstein described time as a "tool invented by man to measure the movement of things" and said, "past, present and future are an illusion, although a persistent one."

Instead, let's think of time as a huge circle, with all the past, present and future inside it. Everything known and unknown is also inside the circle. This concept gives the out-of-body traveler a scientific understanding of why we can see past or future events while out of body.

Einstein also explained that anything composed of atoms that approaches the speed of light will slow down. Once at the speed of light, it will completely stop moving. Therefore, an astronaut traveling at the speed of light would never age, while we on Earth would continue to age because our atoms are vibrating at a different rate.

I believe that when we are out of body, our vibrations change, enabling us to tap into the circle, seeing past, present or future. In fact, I was so profoundly affected by the absence of time on the Other Side that I could no longer wear a watch when I came back to life.

If you still have a hard time with this "no time" concept, you may want to enroll in a beginning physics class at your local college to understand this concept more clearly. I personally believe that when scientists are able to capture the energy that leaves the body during a near-death or out-of-body experience, they'll discover that the spirit can travel at the speed of light.

Einstein's theory of relativity may, in fact, explain why out-of-body travel seems to be instantaneous. If the spirit is able to travel at the speed of light, this might account for the millions of near-death experiencers who claim that they traveled through a tunnel at an incomprehensible speed. It might also account for the consistent reports from returning near-death experiencers that there is no time on the Other Side.

If the spirit travels at the speed of light, it will transcend "time." Einstein pointed this out by explaining that, if a particle is moving at the speed of light, it has an "energy acknowledgment," or can "see," other particles or objects moving at the same speed. I wonder if the supersonic speed attained by near-death experiencers might also help them to see the Light, if indeed it is traveling at the same speed? Some day, perhaps another Einstein will come along to unravel the mystery.

AFTERWORD

The more we learn about the out-of-body and near-death experience, the less fear we'll harbor regarding these new adventures with their fascinating implications.

More research and communication is needed among physicians, ministers, psychologists, and the experiencers themselves. Most physicians admit that they know very little about out-of-body experiences, although surgeons and emergency room personnel are the most familiar with near-death experiences, such as those reported by cardiac-arrest survivors.

I've personally found that surgeons are less likely to dispute near-death or out-of-body experiences than are psychiatrists or psychologists.

On the other hand, several ministers and priests have shared their own out-of-body experiences with me, always emphasizing how positive and uplifting they were. They admit that the experience was so exhilarating, they look forward to repeating it.

I believe that no one is kept from seeing the Light, even if that person has only a tiny spark of goodness within. And once someone is exposed to the love and wisdom within the Light, every cell and molecule within their being is changed completely.

As we learn to let the Light and our angels come into our dreams, we will become "awakened dreamers." This will bring us intuitive and scientific knowledge and spiritual enlightenment, which the world so desperately seeks. I believe that the near-death and out-of-body experience are keys to this enlightenment—keys that will open the doorway to the wisdom of God.

While I was in the Light, God showed me that we must stop being judgmental. We must also learn to appreciate our lives, love our neighbors, stop wars, end religious bickering, cease conflicts between races, and become accepting of differing opinions. Life is too short for us to spend so much time in a state of dissatisfaction.

Instead, we need to help the world to heal. Love is the answer. Light is the answer. Our love and the Light can truly transform the world.

When we generate love, our dreams become pathways to the Light. Here, we will find that life and death truly are interconnected, and that we can begin to live only when we are unafraid to die.

But before we die, let's give more, learn more, love more, dream more. The time is right. The world is ready for change. The world is ready for peace.

The world is ready for the Light!

MY DREAM JOURNAL OF
OUT-OF-BODY EXPERIENCES

My Dream Journal of
Out-Of-Body Experiences

My Dream Journal of
Out-Of-Body Experiences

MY DREAM JOURNAL OF
OUT-OF-BODY EXPERIENCES

MY DREAM JOURNAL OF
OUT-OF-BODY EXPERIENCES

My Dream Journal of Out-Of-Body Experiences

Dr. Dianne Morrissey would like to hear from readers about their own experiences with out-of-body travel. She is particularly interested in results obtained by using the Seven Keys described in this book.

Readers may write to:

Dr. Dianne Morrissey
P.O. Box 4241
Santa Fe Springs, CA
90670

Appendices

The Life Changes Survey

Charts Reflecting a 1994 Survey of 3,765 Participants

Bibliography

Additional Reading

The Life Changes Survey

After my near-death experience in 1977, I wanted to learn everything I could about others who had had similar experiences. In the years immediately following, I spoke to thousands of people who had left their bodies and returned. I was struck by the fact that the near-death experiencers were far more strongly affected than their colleagues who had left their bodies without being close to death.

I began to recognize that a major difference between the two experiences was the near-death vision of heavenly Light. How, I wondered, could "ordinary" out-of-body travelers experience this as well?

The result was eighteen years of research and teaching of the method described in this book. The following data laid the foundation for the work that has, I'm delighted to report, changed the lives of everyone who has taken these steps and ventured towards the Light.

In 1991, I surveyed 1,607 people who agreed to answer questions about how they had changed after their out-of-body experiences. Included were both out-of-body and near-death experiencers.

I asked my respondents eleven questions designed to discover whether, having returned from the Other Side, they felt accepted by relatives or friends; whether or not they wanted to once again become a part of society after what had happened to them; whether or not they were drawn to making significant career changes, to help society, or to continue their education; whether they considered money a primary reason to select or keep a job; whether they found that they had become more introverted or more extroverted afterwards; and whether, as a result of their experiences, they took more risks, no longer fearing death. Here are the results of my survey.

Overall, the near-death experiencers seemed more strongly affected than their out-of-body colleagues. One unexpected finding was that 87% of those who had had near-death experiences believed that they had successfully incorporated their experiences into their lives, while only 23% of those who had had out-of-body experiences felt they had been socially accepted after their experiences. Indeed, 72% of those who had not been close to death thought the acceptance of their experience into society was unnecessary.

People who had had near-death experiences felt the need to be understood and accepted by others afterward. They also told me that they needed to join society in a much more significant way. Some, like myself, sought that integration through the sharing of their experiences with others.

Near-death experiencers took a long time—from four to ten years—to feel as if they were part of society again. Those who had not been close to death and sought social integration afterward took only about a year to feel socially integrated.

Near-death experiencers were also more likely to want to help society. My statistics showed that 30% felt such a desire, in contrast with 12% of out-of-body experiencers.

A majority of the near-death experiencers, or 64%, had changed careers, compared with only 6% of the out-of-body experiencers.

Only 8% of out-of-body experiencers felt they took more risks afterwards, compared with 32% of those who had "died."

Salary as an important criterion for taking a job also elicited different responses from the two groups. Out-of-body experiencers were influenced by salary 56% of the time; only 15% of those who had been clinically dead found salary a significant consideration for selecting a new job. This figure correlates with those of other researchers, who have found a decrease in materialism in those who have had a near-death experiences.

Results of the introversion/extroversion question proved intriguing. People who had had *either* kind of out-of-body experience tended to become more outgoing afterward. Of those who did not come close to death, 43% felt more extroverted; of those who underwent near-death experiences, an impressive 87% reported feeling noticeably more extroverted. This could be a result of their strong desire to share their experiences with others.

And when people do share them, 93%, or almost all of the near-death experiencers found that their stories were accepted by friends and family. On the other hand, only 64% who had left their bodies without risk of death reported that friends and family had accepted their experiences.

These results underscore the increasing validation that near-death experiences are receiving from the general public. Other out-of-body experiences have not yet reached the same level of acceptance.

About 66% of near-death experiencers were motivated to return for higher education after their brush with death, compared to only three percent of those who had had an out-of-body experience when not close to death.

The most significant aftereffect of both the near-death and the out-of-body experience was the loss of the fear of death. Almost all near-death survivors, or 98%, and 83% of out-of-body experiencers, reported that they had lost their fear of death after their experiences. The percentages are so close that it seems to make little difference whether the out-of-body experience occurs during sleep or after being near death; simply being out-of-body will forever transform a person's fear of dying.

*　*　*　*

Those who have learned how to use the Seven Keys to journey into the Light will regard this survey as a historical document. It reflects the difference in impact between out-of-body and near-death travel before the Keys were available to guide one on one's chosen journey.

Today, the gaps between these two forms of out-of-body experience are narrowing as more travelers begin to take control of their dreams and their out-of-body destinations. And, as the life-changing effects of seeing the Light influence more lives, the world can only reflect this experience and be changed for the better.

Charts Reflecting a 1994 Survey of 3,765 Participants

The following charts depict a survey I took in 1994, in which I polled 3765 students to determine how many people were having experiences similar to my own out-of-body journeys. I was surprised to discover how often others had experienced the same phenomena.

1. The first chart shows how many students had had a near-death or out-of-body experience before attending my class.

The chart then shows the success ratio for students who had never previously had an out-of-body experience. After using my Seven Keys, 34% had had their first out-of-body experience within two weeks of completing my course.

2. The second chart shows that, prior to taking my course, only a small percentage of students had asked a witness if they had moved during the jolt. After attending my class, when they asked a witness what they had seen, students found a significant increase in the recognition of the non-moving jolt. Many of these jolts indicate a return to the body.

3. The third chart shows the phenomena directly associated with out-of-body travel. Many students found it a great relief to learn that their fellow classmates had had similar experiences, particularly with sleep paralysis.

Of particular interest is the bar representing lucid dreaming. Generally about 10% of the population has lucid dreams; however, after using the Seven Keys, the number shot up to 39%.

Near-Death vs.
Out-Of-Body
Statistics

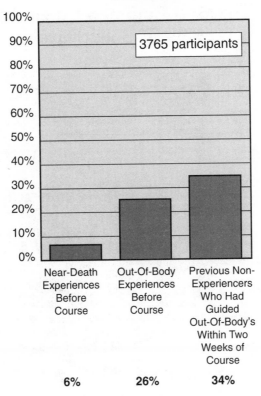

6%	**26%**	**34%**

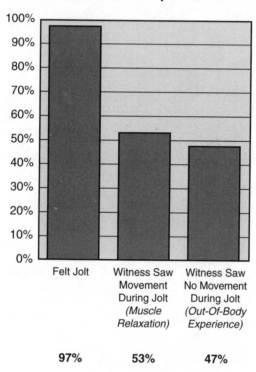

"The Jolt"
The Most Common Experience
for Out-Of-Body Travelers

Other Phenomena associated with Out-Of-Body Experiences

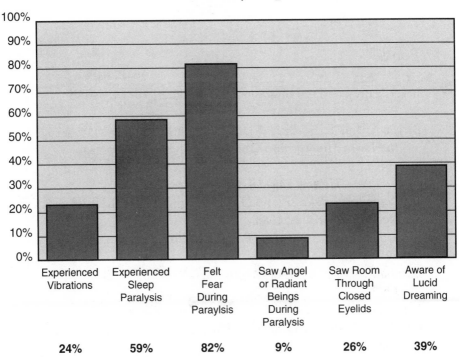

Experienced Vibrations	Experienced Sleep Paralysis	Felt Fear During Paraylsis	Saw Angel or Radiant Beings During Paralysis	Saw Room Through Closed Eyelids	Aware of Lucid Dreaming
24%	**59%**	**82%**	**9%**	**26%**	**39%**

Bibliography

Books

Baker, Jeffrey, and Garland Allen. *Matter, Energy and Life.* Reading, MA.: Addison-Wesley, 1980.

Berger, Arthur S. *Evidence of Life After Death: A Casebook for the Tough Minded.* Springfield, Ill.: Charles C. Thomas, 1988.

Berman, A.L. *Helping Suicidal Adolescents: Needs and Responses, Adolescence and Death.* Corr & J.N. McNeil, Eds. New York: Springer, 1986.

Blackmore, Susan. *Out of the Body?* New York: Prometheus, 1988.

Burnham, Sophy. *A Book of Angels.* New York: Ballantine, 1990.

Capra, Fritjof. *The Tao of Physics.* New York: Bantam, 1977.

Clayman, Charles. *Encyclopedia of Medicine.* New York: Random House, 1989.

Crookall, Robert. *Out-of-Body Experiences.* New York: University Books, 1970.

——*Supreme Adventure.* James Clarke, 1961.

Davidson, Gustav. *A Dictionary of Angels.* New York: Free
Press, 1967.

Descharnes, Robert. *Salvador Dali.* Transl. by Eleanor R. Morse.
New York: Harry N. Abrams, 1976.

——*Dreams and Dreaming and Cosmic Duality.* Alexandria,
Virginia: Time-Life Books, 1990.

Einstein, Albert. *Relativity: The Special and General Theory.*
New York: Henry Holt, 1920.

——*Living Philosophies.* New York: Simon and Schuster,
1931.

Eliot, T.S. *Alfred Lord Tennyson.* New York: Chelsea House,
1985.

Ferm, Vergilius. *The Encyclopedia of Religion.* Secaucus, N.J.:
Poplar Books, 1987.

Fuller, R. Buckminster. *Critical Path.* New York: St. Martin's,
1981.

Gallup, George Jr. *Adventures in Immortality.* New York:
McGraw-Hill, 1982.

Hall, Edward. *The Dance of Life.* New York: Anchor Books/
Doubleday, 1984.

Herberman, Charles, ed. *Catholic Encyclopedia.* New York:
Encyclopedia Press, 1913.

Hinnells, John. *Dictionary of Religions.* Harmondsworth,
Middlesex, England: Penguin, 1984.

Johnson, Thomas H., ed. *Final Harvest: Emily Dickinson's Poems.*
Boston: Little Brown, 1957.

Jung, Carl. *Memories, Dreams, Reflections.* New York:
Pantheon, 1963.

Kastenbaum, Robert, and Beatrice Kastenbaum. *Encyclopedia of
Death.* New York: Avon Books, 1989.

Kastenbaum, Robert, and Ruth Aisenberg. *The Psychology of
Death.* New York: Springer, 1972.

Kubler-Ross, Elisabeth. *To Live Until We Say Goodbye.*
Englewood Cliffs, N.J.: Prentice-Hall, 1978.

The Holy Bible. King James Version. Iowa Falls, Iowa: World
Bible Publishers, N.D.

La Berge, Stephen. *Lucid Dreaming.* Los Angeles: Jeremy P.
Tarcher, 1981.

Lamberg, Lynne. *Guide to Better Sleep.* New York: Random
House, 1984.

Lieberman, Jacob. *Light Medicine of the Future.* Santa Fe, New
Mexico: Bear & Company, 1991.

Mialon, Elly. *The Great Pharaoh Ramses II and His Time.*
Montreal, Canada: Canada Exim Group Quebec, 1985.

Moody, Raymond. *Life After Life.* Harrisburg, PA: Stackpole
Books, 1975.

————*Reflections on Life After Life.* New York: Guideposts,
1977.

————*The Light Beyond.* London: Macmillan, 1988.

Morse, Melvin. *Closer to the Light.* New York: Villard, 1990.

————*Transformed by the Light.* New York: Ivy, 1992.

Muldoon, Sylvan, and Hereward Carrington. *The Projection of
the Astral Body.* Maine: Samuel Weiser, 1982.

O'Connell, Rev. John P. *Holy Bible Challoner Text Dictionary.*
Catholic Press, Chicago: 1958.

Reinhold, Van Nostrand. *Nocturnal Dreaming.* New York: B.B.
Wolman, l979.

Ring, Kenneth. *Life at Death.* New York: Coward, McCann &
Geoghegan, 1980.

————*Heading Toward Omega.* New York: William Morrow,
1984.

Ritchie, George. *The Near-Death Experience.* New York:
Anthroposophic Press, 1992.

Ritchie, George G. *Return From Tomorrow.* Old Tappan, New
Jersey: Chosen Books, 1978.

Shakespeare, William. *The Complete Works of William Shakespeare.* New York: Avenel Books, 1975.

Simonton, Carl. *Getting Well Again.* Los Angeles: Jeremy P. Tarcher, 1978.

Swedenborg, Emanuel. *Heaven & Hell.* New York: Swedenborg Foundation, 1982.

Wagner, Richard. *My Life.* Cambridge, Mass.: Cambridge University Press, 1983.

Walker, Benjamin. *Beyond the Body.* London: Routledge & Kegan Paul, 1977.

Zaleski, Carol. *Otherworld Journeys.* New York: Oxford University Press, 1987.

Periodicals

Isaac Asimov, "Experiment Confirms Kekul's Dream," *Los Angeles Times* (September 16, 1988): Part V.

Susan Blackmore, "Are Out-of-Body Experiences Evidence for Survival?" *Anabiosis: the Journal for Near-Death Studies* (December 1983).

Elizabeth Bodner, ed. "Technicolor Vision," *American Kennel Club Puppies* (1994): 23.

John Boslough, "The Riddle of Time," *Reader's Digest* (December, 1990): 53-56.

Sarah Boxer. "Inside of Sleeping Minds," *Modern Maturity* (October- November 1989): 48-54.

Committee of the Harvard Medical School, "Definition of Brain Death," *Journal of American Medical Association,* (1968): Vol. 205, 337-40. Emily Williams Cook, "Fear of Death Experience," *Omni* (1984).

Amy Sunshine Genova, "The Near-Death Experience," *McCall's* (February, 1988): 103-106.

Andrew Greeley, "The 'Impossible': It's Happening," *American Health Partners* (February, 1987): 7-9.

George Greenstein, "Newton, Einstein and Schwarzschild," *The Key Reporter* (Winter 1984-85): 2-4.

Bruce Greyson, "Near-Death Experiences and Attempted Suicide and Life Threatening Behavior," *ReVision* (November 1981): 1016.

———"Increase in Psychic Phenomena Following Near-Death Experiences," *Theta* (November, 1983): 26-29.

———"A Typology of Near-Death Experiences," *American Journal of Psychiatry* (August, 1985): 8.

Calvin Hall, "Wagnerian Dreams," *Psychology Today* (January, 1983): 34-39.

Myles Harris, "Out of the Body," *The Spectator* (December 10, 1988): 9-11.

Elisabeth Kubler-Ross, "To Be Whole Again," *Parade* (August 11, 1991): 10-12.

Stephen Laberge, "Dr. Dreams," *Los Angeles Times* (November 15, 1988): Part V.

Michael Long, "What is This Thing Called Sleep?" *National Geographic* (December 1987): 787-821.

Los Angeles Times, "Crib Death Linked to Lack of REM Sleep," *Los Angeles Times* (August 23, 1987): Part II.

A. Mcphee, "Kids Who Almost Died," *Current Science* (January 4, 1991): 4-5.

Mary Ann O'Roark, "Life After Death: The Growing Evidence," *Reader's Digest* (August, 1981): 51-55.

Kenneth Ring, "Near-Death Experiences: Implications for Human Evolution and Planetary Transformations," *ReVision* (Winter-Spring, 1986): Vol 8, Number 2.

_____,"Near-Death Experiences," *New Realities* (March/April 1985): 65-70.

Charles Tart, "Lucid Dreams and Out-of-Body Experiences," *The Open Mind* (Winter 1986): Vol. 3, Number 3.

Additional Reading

Books

Anderson, George. *We Don't Die.* New York: Berkeley Books, 1988.

Atwater, P.M.H. *Coming Back to Life.* New York: Ballantine Books,1988.

Bach, Richard. *Bridge Across Forever.* New York: Morrow, 1984.

Barrett, W. *Death-Bed Visions.* London: Methuen, 1926.

Basforth, Terry. *The Near-Death Experience: An Annotated Bibliography.* New York: Garland Publishing, 1990.

Battersby, Prevost. *Man Outside Himself.* London: Rider, 1969.

Bayless, Raymond. *The Other Side of Death.* New York: University Books, 1971.

Bluebond-Langner, Myra. *The Private Worlds of Dying Children.* Princeton, N.J.: Princeton University Press, 1978.

Bramblett, John. *When Good-bye is Forever: Learning to Live Again after the Loss of a Child.* New York: Ballantine, 1991.

Ducasse, C.J. *The Belief in Life After Death.* Springfield, Ill.: Charles C. Thomas, 1961.

Evans-Wentz, W.Y. *The Tibetan Book of the Dead.* New York: Oxford University Press, 1960.

Feifel, Herman. *New Meanings of Death.* New York: McGraw-Hill,1977.

Flynn, Charles. *After the Beyond.* Englewood Cliffs, N.J., Prentice-Hall, 1986.

Flynn, Charles, and Bruce Greyson. *The Near-Death Experiencer: Problems, Prospects, Perspectives.* Springfield, Ill.: Charles C. Thomas, 1984.

Gabbard, Glen, and Stuart Tremlow. *An Empiric Analysis of Out-of-Body States.* New York: Praeger, 1984.

Grof, Stanislav and Christina. *Beyond Death.* England: Thames & Hudson, 1980.

————*The Human Encounter with Death.* New York: E.F. Dutton, 1977.

Grosso, Michael. *The Final Choice.* Walpole, N.H.: Stillpoint, 1985.

Kutscher, Austin. *Death and Bereavement.* Springfield, Ill.: Charles C. Thomas, 1969.

Levine, Stephen. *Meetings at the Edge: Dialogues with the Grieving and the Dying, the Healing and the Healed.* New York: Doubleday, 1984.

Matson, A. *Afterlife.* Tempo Books, 1976.

Mitchell, Janet. *Out-of-Body Experiences.* Jefferson, N.C.: McFarland, 1981.

Monroe, Robert. *Journeys Out of the Body;* New York: Doubleday, 1977.

————*Far Journeys.* New York: Doubleday, 1987.

Muldoon, Sylvan, and Hereward Carrington. *The Projection of the Astral Body.* Maine: Samuel Weiser, 1982.

Osis, Karlis. *At the Hour of Death.* New York: Avon, 1977.

Parish-Harra, C. *A New Age Handbook on Death and Dying.* Marina del Ray, CA.: DeVorss, 1982.

Rawlings, M. *Beyond Death's Door.* Nashville: Thomas Nelson, 1978.

Sabom, Michael. *Recollections of Death: A Medical Investigation.* New York: Harper & Row, 1982.

Shirley, Ralph. *The Mystery of the Human Double.* London: Rider, 1972.

Smith, Susy. *The Enigma of Out-of-Body Travel.* New York: Helix Press, 1965.

Sorensen, Michelle. *The Journey Beyond Life.* Orem, Utah: Family Affair, 1988.

Thompson, Robert J. *The Proofs of Life after Death.* Werner Laurie, 1902.

Von Franz, Marie-Louise. *On Dreams and Death.* Boston, MA.: Shambhala, 1987.

Zaleski, Carol. *Otherworld Journeys: Accounts of Near-Death Experience in Medieval and Modern Times.* New York: Oxford University Press, 1987.

Periodicals

D. Corcoran, "Helping Patients Who've Had Near-Death Experiences," *Nursing* (November, 1988).

Sarah Sheets Cook, "Children and Dying: An Exploration and Selective Bibliographies," *Health Sciences Pub.* (1974).

P. Giovetti, "Near-Death and Deathbed Experiences: An Italian Survey," *Theta* (October, 1982).

R. Kohr, "Near-Death Experience and Its Relationship to Psi and Various Altered States," *Theta* (1982).

———Los Angeles Times, "A Step Toward the Light," *Los Angeles Times* (September 18, 1990): E1.

"After "Near-Death" Atheist Yields Slightly on Afterlife," *Los Angeles Times* (October 8, 1988): Part II.

R. J. Noyes, "Attitude Change Following Near-Death Experiences," *Psychiatry* (1980): 234-242.

Karlis Osis, "Deathbed Observations by Physicians and Nurses," *Parapsychological Foundation Inc.* (1961).

Stuart Tremlow, Glen Gabbard, and Fowler Jones, "The Out-of-Body Experience: II Phenomenology," *Paper delivered at meeting of American Psychiatric Association* (1980).

S. Vicchio, "Near-Death Experiences: A Critical Review of the Literature and Some Questions for Further Help," *Anabiosis* (January, 1981).

For ADDITIONAL INFORMATION, you may wish to pursue other works offering alternative approaches. One of the earliest works frequently referred to is *Heaven and Hell* by Emanuel Swedenborg, born 1688; died 1772. Nearly two hundred years later came *The Projection of the Astral Body* in 1929, by Sylvan J. Muldoon and Hereward Carrington, followed by the books of Robert Crookall, Ph.D., especially *The Study and Practice of Astral Projection* in 1966. Research by Elisabeth Kubler-Ross, M.D., led to *On Death and Dying* in 1969, followed by Raymond Moody Jr., M.D. with *Life After Life* in 1975 and *Reflections on Life after Life* in 1977. Psychological aspects of the near-death experiencer were offered in *Life At Death* in 1980 and *Heading Toward Omega* by Kenneth Ring, Ph.D., in 1984.

For other fine Stillpoint materials that awaken the human spirit, may we recommend:

6 x 9 1/2 display case
224 page illustrated hardcover book
48 magnificent full-color cards
ISBN: 0-913299-95-2 $29.95

Angelic Messenger Cards
A Divination System for Spiritual Self-Discovery
BY MEREDITH YOUNG-SOWERS

A classic in its own time! These gorgeous cards and powerful angelic messages will help you connect with your angels and your own inner wisdom.

5 3/4 x 9, Cloth
288 pages
ISBN: 1-883478-05-7
$18.95

Teachings from the Angelic Messenger Cards
BY MEREDITH YOUNG-SOWERS

A fascinating system to record your responses to the special angelic messages you receive from the Angelic Messenger Cards. Set new goals to improve all your relationships. Learn how to give angelic energy readings, track the Angelic Messenger Cards you've drawn from the previous month, and use intuitive journaling to find your own answers.